D1373197

The Dedicated Life

The Dedicated Life

BY THE

REV. F. B. MEYER, B.A.

AMBASSADOR

BELFAST   **GREENVILLE**
NORTHERN IRELAND   SOUTH CAROLINA

The Dedicated Life

This edition 1997

ISBN   1 898787 88 3

AMBASSADOR PRODUCTIONS LTD,
Providence House
16 Hillview Avenue,
Belfast, BT5 6JR
Northern Ireland

Emerald House,
1 Chick Springs Road, Suite 206
Greenville,
South Carolina 29609
United States of America

CONTENTS

———◆———

THE DEDICATED LIFE

———◆———

I.

THE DEDICATED LIFE.

THE theme of the Epistle to the Romans is the memorable sentence of the Prophet Habakkuk, " The just shall live by faith." The importance and depth of those words is clearly evidenced in the fact that they are quoted three times in the New Testament, as the final court of appeal. Setting them on the forefront of this great treatise, the Apostle has already through eleven chapters expanded and beaten out the various implications of *faith*. " A propitiation through *faith* in His Blood " : " To Abraham his *faith* was reckoned for righteousness " : " Therefore being justified by *faith*," etc. He has wrought up the successive stages of his argument to three crowning conclusions (v. 21 ; viii. 39 ; xi. 36). And now he turns to develop the full significance of *live* : " The just by his faith shall *live*." In chapters xii. and xiii. he shows what kind of life that is which results from faith in the Son of God, *first* in the *religious* (xii.) and then in the *civil* (xiii.) sphere. (Hab. ii. 4 ; Rom. i. 17; Gal. iii. 11 ; Heb. x. 38.)

There are two spheres in which each of us is called to live. These are the inner circle of our Church relationship and the outer of relationship to the community or State. It is not enough to lay down the general principles of sanctified life, leaving their application to the individual soul, because our

consciences are so warped by the false standards to which we have become habituated
from childhood upwards. It is necessary to
educate conscience by setting before it the
standards of the Kingdom of God. A deaf
and dumb child, living always among people
similarly afflicted, would need very careful
instruction before it could, from lip-language,
acquire the accent and tone of perfect arti-
culation. The child of peasant ancestry is
long before it can acquire the habits of the
Court. They say that a foreigner never
speaks with the precise accuracy of the native-
born children of the race and country which
he adopts. So there must be line on line, and
precept on precept of careful instruction,
before the saint realises all the implications
of the new life, which, originating in the spirit,
works out through soul and body into the
perfect beauty of the Divine ideal.

The tenderness of the Apostle's appeal. " I

beseech you." It is a favourite word with him. He never claimed lordship over his converts. There were times when, in correcting abuses, his spirit was hot with indignation and he did not spare ; but for the most part he was winsome and gentle among them, " as when a nurse cherisheth her own children." At one time he based his tender entreaty on the sorrows of his imprisonment ; at another, on the weight of his accumulating years ; at another, on the tender love he bore them. But the wooing note is characteristic of the man who, amid all the strife and contention of his life, never lost the savour of "the meekness and gentleness of Christ."

Its basis. " I beseech you, *therefore, by the mercies of God.*" What mercies ? Not only the mercy of xi. 30 ; but those great mercies on which he had been dilating in the opening chapters of this Book. The word *present* is, of course, the same as we have in

vi. 19, and carries us back to the sublime
arguments that deal with the basis of our
faith. Indeed, some have even hazarded the
suggestion that chapters vii. to xi. are a prolonged parenthesis ; and that, returning from
his digression, the Apostle proceeds on the
line of thought introduced by the abrupt
question of vii. 1. The word *therefore*, in
fact, gathers up the whole doctrinal part of
the Epistle ; and " the mercies of God "
include not only our creation, preservation,
and all the blessings of this life, but, above
all, God's inestimable love in the redemption
of our race—the means of grace and the hope
of glory. The mercy of the eternal choice ;
the mercy of the Divine way of righteousness ;
the mercy of peace through the Blood of the
Cross ; the mercy of the new Headship of our
race through the Second Adam ; the mercy of
identification in the death and resurrection
of our Lord. In one of the Psalms the singer,

in an ecstasy, cried that the sacrifice should
be bound with cords " even unto the horns of
the altar" (Ps. cxviii. 27). The abundant
salvation he had experienced set him singing.
The twisted cords of God's intertwining
mercies, woven into one strong, sufficient cable,
hold us to the altar of sacrifice. We can
do no other. The Love of Christ constrains
us, the Spirit of Christ masters us, the Grace
of Christ holds us spellbound, steadfast, and
unmovable. From henceforth, let no man
trouble us. Christ, and Christ only, is our
passion.

It is on the basis of Christ's finished work
that we surrender ourselves to God. We do
not work up to salvation; but down from it.
We do not serve to be saved; but being
saved, we serve. We have received the
Reconciliation, and now enjoy God's finished
salvation *imputed* to us in Christ, and *imparted* to us, in germ by the Spirit, to bear

ultimately the flowers and fruits of holy living. It cannot be too carefully insisted that the life described in these two chapters is only possible to those who realise their oneness with Him who was crucified, dead, and buried, and who rose from the dead the third day according to the Scriptures. It is because of the Sacrifice unto Death, once offered on the Cross, that we are called to make this Sacrifice unto Life, in all the activities of the Church and the world. "Present yourselves unto God, as alive from the dead, and your members as instruments of righteousness unto God."

Our attitude to that basis. Before we go farther, let us ask whether these great truths are properly apprehended by us. The Christian religion differs from other religions in this, that it consists not in a number of doctrines to be believed or rites to be practised, but in the union of the soul with Him of whom we are told that He was "delivered up for our offences and was raised again for out justification."

We are not united to Him by the tenure of doctrine or the observance of ritual, but by faith. Faith is the act of our spirit, quickened by the Spirit of God, whereby a definite union is effected between us and Christ. It begins often in a sense of need, in a yearning for help, in the reaching out of our dumb, blind hands, feeling after Him if haply we may find Him, in a cry as of a child in the dark, in the definite appeal to Him for help and salvation, in the casting ourselves out of ourselves on Him, in the dropping into the void to find ourselves caught by His everlasting arms.

You may believe what you will *about* Him, but you are invited to believe in (or, as the Greek puts it, *into*) Him. There must be the adhesion of the nature to the Divine Lord, as of the branch grafted into the tree. Faith is the power of receptivity. It is the open door and open window on the south side of the house of the soul, so that the light and warmth of the Eternal Sun may be wafted to us. In that union with the Living Christ is salvation, and nowhere else. Directly *it is formed, the tides of His Eternal Life* begin to invade and pour into the soul of man as the waters of the brimming ocean into the opened estuary.

II.

THE REGIMEN OF THE BODY.

" Present your bodies . . ."

ST. FRANCIS of Assisi, when dying, looked down on his emaciated and suffering body, and said, in grim pity, " I've been hard on my poor brother, the ass." It was as though his body had been the humble companion and burden-bearer of his soul's pilgrimage in the daily trudge of their common life. Such a sentiment, however, was in clear advance of the monastic conception of the age, which despised the body as the source of sin and believed salvation to be only possible through systematic and painful austerity.

10

Prolonged fastings, cruel scourgings, the hair shirt, were the only pathway to salvation.

So absorbing were the demands of this dualistic theory that its proselytes sank to the level of wild beasts. Hermits abandoned their clothing, resorted to the lairs of wild animals, and went about naked with shaggy and disordered hair. In Mesopotamia a sect arose who lived by eating grass. They had no dwellings, and ate neither bread nor vegetables, but wandered on the hills and fed on herbage. Cleanliness of body was regarded with disfavour, as indicating corruption of soul, and the most venerated of the saints were those who took no care of their bodies. Athanasius, for instance, relates with approval that St. Anthony never washed his feet.

The result so far as the physical degeneration of the foremost races of that age is concerned is evident in the Art of the period. " If," says M. Taine, " one considers the

stained-glass windows or the images in the
cathedrals, or the rude paintings, it appears as
if the human race had become degenerate
and its blood had become impoverished.
Pale saints, distorted martyrs, virgins with
flat chests, feet too long and bony hands,
hermits withered and unsubstantial, Christs
that look like crushed and bleeding earth-
worms, processions of figures that are wan,
stiffened, and sad, upon whom are stamped
all the deformities of misery, and all the
shrinking timidity of the oppressed—such
were the results of the distorted doctrines of
that time."

This was not in the Apostle's thought when
he urged his converts to present their bodies
to God. He could not have sympathised
with the unfortunate A.V. translation of Phil.
iii. 21, where the body is described as *vile*.
The Greek phrasing should of course be
rendered as in R.V., " the body of our humilia-

tion." We should of course hold for God, and surrender to His use, bodies in the most perfect health and fitness possible, that they may perform the longest and the best service of which they are capable.

As the olden worshippers thought it shame to bring for sacrifice the blind, the lame, and the sick, so should we endeavour to bring to our life-work unimpaired health, glad spirits, patience under long-continued strain, and the precious endowment of deep child-like sleep. These are the invaluable assets of the Christian worker. Keep your body in good health!

Of course, where there is some physical thorn in the flesh, with its constant suffering and deformity, we must count on a greater abundance of Divine strength, and not flinch from our life-task. But, speaking generally, it is through healthy bodies that the best work of the world is done. Sydney Smith confessed that he had eaten and drunk,

between his seventh and seventieth year,
more than forty-four waggon-loads of food
in excess of his real needs : and perhaps this
was the cause of the vicious spleen which he
infused into his writings, like the ink with
which the cuttlefish discolours the ocean.

What a bicycle is to the cyclist, the body
is in the race of life. However strong or
clever the competitor for the championship
may be, he will stand no chance if his wheel
is out of order. And we make life much more
difficult for ourselves and others if we defile
our bodies by sinful excess, or undermine
their vigour by disregard of the laws of
health.

But the body must never usurp the highest
place in our thought. Even recreation must
be subordinated to our life purpose. The
Apostle said, " I keep under my body."
That is its proper place. Its interests must
never predominate in our economy. The

stable-boy can never be allowed to dictate the policy of the royal castle over which the standard is waving. Whenever any sensual indulgence arises and demands exclusive attention, it must be ordered " to heel," and kept there by the grace of Christ.   With some the life-temptation may lie in their inordinate love of eating and drinking ; with others. over-indulgence may be solicited in regard to tobacco, alcohol, or the parental instinct ; with others again, there is too exclusive an absorption in pleasure.   We are quick to see these failings in others, let us judge ourselves !

After all, next to the grace of God, nothing will help us so much to keep our body and its various organs and instincts in their right place, as to use it for the highest and noblest ends, and that is surely in the Apostle's mind when he bids us present our bodies to God as living sacrifices.   It would seem as though he went back again on the argument of the sixth chapter, and urged that as the members had been yielded as instruments of unrighteousness to sin, so now they should be yielded with equal earnestness to God as instruments of righteousness and holiness. It is not for us to be always on the alert to initiate our own life-courses, as though the origin and fountain of life lay with ourselves; we must believe that God's Spirit is within, inspiring, suggesting, and impelling, and that all we have to do is to give Him right of way.

This was so with our Lord. As the Second Person in the Holy Trinity, He presented Himself to the Father that the creative purpose might work through Him. Through the ages as they passed He was always presenting Himself to the Father that His providential purposes might be realised through Him. When He stooped to the manger-cradle it was that the Father's Name and Character

should be revealed through Him ; and when
death was behind, and the grave rent, and
the shackles with which the Devil sought to
bind Him lay at His feet in pieces, He presented
Himself to God, that through Him God might
work out His entire redeeming purpose, bring-
ing in the everlasting kingdom, which is
righteousness, joy, and peace.

It is in a similar manner that we are to bring
our natures to God, not for death, but for life,
and for ever fuller life. We were purchased
for this by the precious blood, we have been
prepared for it by ceaseless care, now let us
reverently, humbly, prayerfully, and gladly
yield ourselves to God. He will not only
work through us for that which is more
specially and distinctively religious, but
through all the avenues of our existence that
He may realise in us the most perfect type of
manhood or womanhood of which we are
capable.

III.

GOD'S WILL IN DAILY DUTY.

THE will of God is goodwill. Some
people seem to think that it stands for
whatever would limit, depress, and sadden
human life. There is a hymn which I absolutely refuse to make use of in public worship,
because in successive verses it reflects this
spirit. One stanza may be quoted as a fair
specimen of the rest :—

> " If Thou shouldst call me to resign
> What most I prize, it ne'er was mine :
> I only yield Thee what was Thine.
> Thy will be done."

It is quite true that when the will of God
comes into collision with our habitual prefer-

ences and tastes we shall experience the
bitterness of the Cross as we renounce them
and yield ourselves to its drastic pruning.
But if we could know as well as God does
what is best, we should be the first to rejoice
that He has taken pains to rid us of the can-
cerous growth that must have ultimately de-
stroyed us. If a man will but live wholly and
utterly, in thought and word and deed, in the
will of God, you will have one who is antici-
pating heaven, and whose life is the broadest,
freest, and gladdest that it is possible to live.
If God's will were done on earth as it is done
in heaven, earth would become heaven. Do
not fear the will of God, but fear to live outside
of it, for " it is good, acceptable, and perfect."

It is *Good*. No taint of evil or impurity
can live in its pure atmosphere. It is like
the air of the high Alps, in which microbes
of corruption and disease cannot exist. Those
who live in it perfectly are without fault

before the throne of God. Into their hearts
there can enter nothing that worketh abomination or maketh a lie.

It is *Acceptable*. The impression produced
on those who are unprejudiced, when they
come in contact with a life lived only for the
will of God, is that it is beautiful, it attracts
them, it is acceptable. Our service is acceptable and well-pleasing to God; and His will,
as we begin to live in it and practise it, makes
us men and women of His good pleasure.

It is *Perfect*. There is nothing beyond it.
When we have realised it even in our poor
measure, we know the joy that is unspeakable
and the peace that passes understanding. If
we travel back to the time before the world
was, we can only imagine that perfect peace,
perfect joy, and perfect love reigned supreme
in that past eternity, as we believe that they
will reign supreme for ever. And why?
Because the will of God was done. Whence

have come the sorrow, pain, and anguish that mar human life to-day? From rebellion against the will of God. And the Father can only wipe away tears from off all faces by winning us back to love and to do His will. "The world passeth away, and the lust thereof, but he that doeth the will of God abideth for ever."

As we turn over the pages of the Gospels we find underlying them all the perpetual sounding of this note of perfect harmony with the will of God. In the words of the Psalmist, our Lord could say, "In the volume of the book it is written of Me, I delight to do Thy will, O my God." The perpetual motive of our Saviour's life was the doing of the Father's will. As a boy in His mother's home, or a carpenter in Joseph's shop, in the Jordan waters, or on the Mount of Temptation, when working miracles or hastening to Calvary—wherever He was and whatever He was doing there was the same sweet music.   Once only in the life of the race has a human life been perfectly conformed to the will of God, but that life was perfectly blessed, running over with peace and joy.   " My *peace* I give unto you "—" that My *joy* may remain in you, and that your joy may be full."   As Dante puts it, " In His will is our peace."

The happiness of life consists, then, in obeying two conditions.   First, *we must receive all things from the will of God*, and dare to believe, however their appearance seems to contradict our faith, that they are good, acceptable, and perfect.   Secondly, *we must in all things do the will of God, so far as we can discern it*; and as we do so, it will become clearer and dearer, and its thread will lead us through life's obscure labyrinthine passages into the perfect daylight of eternity.   " Teach me to do Thy will, for Thou art my God ; Thy Spirit is good, lead me into the land of uprightness."   The ox between plough

and altar is the true emblem of our lives.
To be ready for either—to be willing to bear
the yoke over the barren furrows, or to do
God's will till we are brought to the Cross,
is the key to the perennial fountains of life.

God's will is only forbidding to those who
look at it to refuse it. If it is accepted, it
becomes good, acceptable, and perfect to the
soul. It must be so, because God is a faithful
Creator, and has adapted our nature to its
true environment, as birds to the air, and
web-footed animals to the water. He also
is love, and could not contemplate an eternal
disharmony in those whom He called into
existence. He is the God and Father of our
Lord Jesus Christ, and we may find in Him
all that Jesus did in His earthly life, when He
said, " My meat is to do the will of Him that
sent Me, and to finish His work."

Our minds become perpetually renewed
(1) by daily meditation on the Will of God;

(2) by daily accepting all things from it; (3) by daily obeying all things which it bids. Just as the motor needs to be constantly recharged, so do our minds require every day to be brought into living contact with God's Word; and as we do so we become transfigured into the likeness of the Son of God, and we increasingly realise how good and acceptable the will of God is. Oh, do not suffer one day to pass without coming into assenting contact with God's will, choose, and do it, so you will come to love it.

Daily life affords our supreme opportunity for this daily contact. The old masters in painting may have known how to mix their colours, but they gave men a wrong conception of religion. In their pictures you will see men and women in every stage of emaciation and misery, in convent cells or cathedral stalls, absolutely divorced from natural human life, with the aureoles of saintship around their heads. Ruskin's comment on Raphael's great cartoon of " The Miraculous Draught of Fishes " is so apposite, that we wonder it did not occur to the painter himself. " Here are the Apostles, dressed as ecclesiastics, looking most magnificent, though they had toiled all the night ! "   It is founded on a false conception !

> " The parish priest of austerity
>   Climbed up in the high church-steeple
> To be nearer God, so that he might
>   Hand His Word down to the people.
> And in sermon script he daily wrote
>   What he thought was sent from heaven ;
> And he dropped it down on the people's heads
>   Two times one day in seven.
> In His rage God said, ' Come *down* and die ' ;
>   And he cried out from the steeple,
> ' Where art Thou, Lord ? '   And the Lord replied,
>   ' Down here among My people.' "

This is what Paul teaches.   God is down here among common folk and ordinary circumstances, and His will is concerned in the daily duties of our lives.   Let us gird ourselves to find it and do it *there* !

IV.

THE TRANSFIGURED LIFE.

THE Transfiguration from some aspects may be described as a conspicuous climax in our Lord's ministry. It took place on one of the lower slopes of Hermon, in the neighbourhood of which He was spending a few days with the Apostles, as though girding up His soul for the crowning culmination of His redeeming purpose on the Cross—only six months distant. Night had probably settled on the mountains when this transcendent experience befell Him. It was His custom to spend nights in prayer alone, but on this occasion the little group of friends that were often admitted to His closest in-

26

timacy were with Him by special invitation,
and they were permitted to behold that great
sight when the glory of His spiritual body
threatened to steal over and envelop His
person.

We must not compare the glory that
emanated from Christ's person, and made
His face to shine as the sun, with that which
shone on the face of Moses. The latter was a
transient reflection of the glory he had beheld
during his sojourn with God on the mount,
but the light that enwreathed our Lord was
the Shekinah glory which dwelt always in
His heart, as of old within the Tabernacle
(John i. 14). For the most part it was strictly
curtained, but on this occasion it burst forth
like a fountain that rushes up from some hidden
source with irresistible energy and refuses
to brook restraint. Remember that this
happened as He prayed. Even His garments
of common homespun were saturated, and

became glistening as when sunlight falls on snow—an emblem this of the way in which the love and power of God, as the result of secret prayer, may glorify the meanest and commonest wrappings of our human life.

There is little doubt that from this moment of glory our Lord might have stepped back into heaven. Death is associated with sin, and since our Lord was sinless, He might have suddenly been changed in a moment. In the twinkling of an eye His mortality might have been swallowed up of life. Yet, if this had been the case, though He might have been the Patron He could never have been the Saviour of mankind. He knew that nothing less than the shedding of His life-blood could meet the awful need of the world, and therefore He resolutely turned His back on the open door of Paradise, and the bosom of the Father whence He had proceeded,

refused to heed the voices that bade Him
spare Himself, and deliberately set His face
towards the Cross. There, at the end of
the cypress-lined path, it stood with open
arms as though to embrace Him; and instead of the joy that was set before Him
" He set His face stedfastly to go to Jerusalem." He knew all things that were ap-
pointed for Him to suffer, but deliberately
chose them because only so could He achieve
our salvation.

The mighty Law-giver of Sinai and the
Prophet of Fire, who came to stand beside
the Lord, represented the Law and the
Prophets, and bore witness to the power of
Jesus over other worlds and orders of beings
than ourselves. He holds the key of Death
and of Hades. When He unlocked the gates
even these mighty spirits came at His call.
Vast issues were impending, and aware of
the tragedy of sorrow and pain through which

their Master was about to pass, they came to strengthen His human nature for the experiences through which He was to come to His throne. The sheen of glory awoke the Apostles in time to behold that radiant Trio and that dazzling cloud which settled down upon them, and to hear the Voice that declared how the love of eternity had existed unbroken amid time-relations, and that their Master was Son of the Highest in a unique and unapproachable sense.

All this must have been present to the mind of the Apostle when he said, beneath the inspiration of the Divine Spirit, " Be not conformed to this world, but be ye transformed." The Greek word is the same as is used of the transfiguration of the Lord. (See also 2 Cor. iii. 18.) And we may in our degree learn that the salient features of the Transfiguration may be repeated in miniature in our little lives, as once I saw the mighty

Matterhorn reflected in a tiny lakelet, fifteen miles distant.

We are often bidden to resist those strong attractions that fasten human souls to the passing evanescent conditions which surround them. " Arise ye, and depart, for this is not your rest," is ever ringing like a clarion in our ears. But how can we obey the Divine summons for detachment unless we are forming habits of attachment ? How can we resist the flux and drift of the tide, unless like the sea anemone we can adhere to the everlasting rocks ? In other words, we can only get free from the assimilating influences of time and the world in proportion as we are transfigured *by the renewing of our mind*. The light that came on the face of our Lord was not from without but from within ; it broke out from a hidden furnace of love. So it shall be with us. As we view the supreme sacrifice of our Saviour to the death, and

endeavour to repeat it in our small measure
in the devotement and consecration of our
lives; as day by day we consider the great
claims that He has on us, and prepare to
answer to them; as we offer and present
ourselves, our souls and bodies, in thought
and intention, to be a reasonable, holy, and
living sacrifice unto Him, this growing habit
of our mind will achieve a corresponding
effect upon our whole being.

As a man thinks in his heart so is he, and
as we think of ourselves as living sacrifices,
choosing death, even the death of the cross
as our Lord did, the transfiguring glory of
that high resolve will pass into our faces,
and irradiate our meanest actions. Then
the world with all its fascination will cease
to hold us; then we shall climb the mountain
altars of prayer, and as we pray we shall be
changed; then we shall realise our kinship
with the saints of every age; then the voice

of God will declare us to be His beloved children ; then the heavens around us shall seem more certainly our home than the earth beneath our feet, though we shall turn from its beckoning rapture to the lowly tasks and sacrifices which await us at the foot of the mountain.

The one matter for all of us is to seek continually the renewing of our mind. The cistern soon gets exhausted and must be refilled. The spent energy of nerve and muscle needs to be recuperated by food and sleep, and the soul needs to be restored, the ideals and resolves of the mind require re-invigoration and recharging. These are to be obtained only in fellowship with God through the Word and private prayer and holy fellowship with the saints. Day by day therefore let us seek this renewing of the mind.

V.

SOBER-MINDEDNESS.

ROM. xii. 3.

IN a sermon on this verse, to which we are
indebted, the late H. W. Beecher
remarks that it is very difficult to find ex-
pressions adequate to show the beautiful
play of words which exists in the original.
He quotes Dean Alford as giving the following sentence, which, though a clumsy imita-
tion, may give some idea of the structure of
the original. "Not to be high-minded above
what one ought to be minded, but to be
minded so as to be sober-minded." In all
four places the words are the same, yet so
varied by their inflection as to be in beautiful

gradation and antithesis. Think of self so as
not to over-think ! Think of yourself with
sober, moral judgment, as contrasted with
that reckless, careless state into which one
falls when the influences of truth and conscience are relaxed.

Some men are naturally prone to self-
esteem. It is part of their nature. The
point on which they flatter themselves may be
extremely silly and insignificant, whether of
face, or lace, or place, or even of grace ; but
they are immensely proud of it. It does not
require a large amount of gas to inflate a big
balloon. Not that such people betray themselves in their talk. They are too proud to
expose themselves to the criticism of their
fellows, and often take the lowest seat that
they may be remonstrated with and urged to
go higher. The vain man may be garrulous,
the proud man is generally reticent ; but
his overweening sense of importance

forces itself into notice by a hundred tiny devices.

Other men become self-opinionated because they are surrounded by weak and dwarfed natures, that fawn on them with fulsome flattery, and fail to supply that high standard of character which would effectually reduce their self-estimate to its proper proportions. It is not difficult to think well of ourselves, if only we will measure ourselves by a rule sufficiently lax and low. If you will tamper with the scales, you can make half a pound weigh a pound. It is not difficult to call yourself six feet tall, if you reduce each foot to ten or eleven inches. Lower the standard of your degrees, and every man may become a graduate. It is lamentable for a man when, like James I. of England, he is surrounded by sycophants and flatterers who extol him in the abject phrasing of the Preface to the Authorised Version. Can we wonder that he

presumed to compare criticism of his deeds or
words with blasphemy against Almighty God ?

The witty Frenchman describes this phase
of character as suffering from a swelled head,
but originally it is begotten by a proud and
selfish heart ; and there is no cure for it but
the creation of that contrite and humble heart
which is the supreme gift of Christ. " The
sacrifices of God are a broken spirit ; a broken
and contrite heart, O God, Thou wilt not
despise."

There is a regimen of soul, as we have
already suggested, which will speedily correct
this overweening self-appreciation. Horace
Bushnell, writing of his experiences in London,
says : " The visit was just what I wanted. It
does not crush me or anything like that,
but it shows me what a speck I am. Anything that makes us know the world better,
or our relation to it, the ways of reaching
mankind, what popularity is worth, how large

the world is, and how many things it takes to fill it with an influence—anything that sets a man practically in his place is a mental good."

It is on the same line of thought that the Apostle is arguing here. The Divine Spirit, speaking through him, gives practical direction and advice of the highest value. He says in effect : " Do not be proud, because you possess nothing that you have not received. All the virtues, excellencies, and talents with which your life is furnished have been imparted by the God to whom you must render an account of their employment and culture. " Who maketh thee to differ ? And what hast thou that thou didst not receive ? But if thou didst receive it, why dost thou glory as if thou hadst not received it ? "

But this is not all : the Apostle bids us measure ourselves by the great standard of Faith, which probably stands here for the highest possibilities of the soul in union with God. What have not men done who have become knit through a living faith with the Risen Christ? They have subdued kingdoms, wrought righteousness, obtained the promises, stopped the mouths of lions, quenched the violence of fire; out of weakness have been made strong, have waxed valiant in fight, and turned to flight armies of aliens! Nothing is impossible to faith, which opens a man's soul to the incoming tides of Divine All-Sufficiency. How feeble, how paltry are our lives compared with theirs, whose names are recorded in the annals of the Church! Truly we can only lay claim to a measure, and perhaps to a very inconsiderable measure, of their faith. We are pigmies indeed when we stand beside a Luther, a Knox, a Moody, or a Chalmers!

A village artist was highly flattered by his neighbours and friends, who held his early essays in art to be of incomparable excellence.

Their florid speeches convinced him that he could claim kindred with a Raphael or a Titian, till he paid his first visit to an Art Gallery the walls of which were covered with masterpieces. Then, as he compared his poor daubs with the glowing colour of the immortals, he was overwhelmed with shame and confusion of face, and in the hour of disillusionment vowed that he would never again put brush to canvas. Only afterwards he ventured to reassure himself and resolved to set himself to climb slowly and arduously the ladder to success.

Do not look down to those beneath you, but up to those who tower above in the perfected beauty of Christian character ; do not compare yourself with the poor copies, but with the Divine Original. Turn from the exemplars of faith, furnished by the pages of Scripture, to the Author and Perfecter of Faith Himself. Instead of comparing yourself with yourself, or with your neighbours, compare yourself with the excelling glory of the Divine Redeemer, not only in His blamelessness and spotlessness, but in His love, His devotion, His passion for the salvation of the lost. Do not pit your excellence against other people's failures, but your failures against their virtues. Take into consideration all the advantages and privileges that were within your reach, and of which you have made so poor a use.

It is not only what you are that you must appraise, but what you might have been. Remember your many failures, shortcomings, and sins ! Then you will soon cease to be highminded, you will fear lest you may be a castaway, you will count yourself the least of all saints and the chief of sinners. You will be prepared to take the lowest place ; not undervaluing yourself, not under-estimating your talents or opportunities, not affecting a false humility, but thinking soberly of yourself, and thankfully of what God has done for you and through you, and saying with the Apostle: "By the grace of God I am what I am; and His grace that was bestowed upon me was not in vain."

Thomas à Kempis says: "Oh, how abjectly and meanly ought I to think of myself! How worthless and vain should I deem the good that appeareth to be mine! With what profound humility, O Lord, ought I to cast myself into the abyss of Thy judgments, where I continually find myself to be nothing and nothing! Oh, depth immense! Oh, fathomless and impassable gulf! in which my whole being is absorbed and lost. Where now is the lurking-place of human glory, where the confidence of human virtue? In the awful deep of Thy judgments which covers me, all self-confidence and self-glory are swallowed up for ever!"

VI.

CHRISTIAN SOLIDARITY.

ROM. xii. 4–5.

A WHILE ago, after conducting the usual Morning Prayer with our servants, it suddenly occurred to me how great a difference lay between their lives and mine. To *me* the day seemed to beckon with varied and important engagements, with opportunities for conspicuous usefulness, with those associations with men and things which, to small spheres, seem great; to *them*, there were the common round, the daily task of uneventful and ordinary routine.

Now it is impossible that people should do their best work in the world unless they

have some kind of incentive other than
habit or wages; and I thought that I
might suggest a motive which would give
a new zest to their service. I said, therefore, something like this: "You are asked to
do many things in the house, which we do not
handle, not because there is anything menial
or unworthy in them, but because if we were
to spend our time in doing them, we should
have no chance of performing those services
for which we are specially fitted. We therefore leave these offices which you can do as
well as, or better than, we could, that we may
give ourselves to those other matters which
by God's gift and providence we can do
but you cannot. But when God reckons
with us all at the last, He will allot to *you*
rewards for all the souls you have saved,
the saints you have comforted, the movements
you have inspired; and when you are tempted
to remonstrate and explain that there must be

some mistake, because you have done none
of these things, the Great Father will reply :
' No, it is quite right that these rewards
should come to you, because you set My
servants free and gave them leisure for the
fulfilment of these important functions ; it
is only fair, therefore, to reward you for what
they did in consequence of *your* help, but
could not have done had you not been
faithful and patient.' " This greatly encour-
aged our household servants, and provided
an incentive to more interested service. They
perceived that if they failed in their duty,
so as to cause friction of temper or loss of
time, which hindered and prejudiced our
labour, not only would God's work suffer,
and we lose our reward, but they also would
forfeit some of those eternal and amaranthine
joys that will fall to the share of the faithful
and wise servant. This is solidarity, the word
which stands for common interests, common

efforts, for the success and reward of each, in the co-operation of all. This is the thought of the Apostle in these memorable words, *We are one body in Christ.* Repeatedly in the earlier chapters of the Acts we are told of believers being *added.* It is generally supposed that they were added *to the Church,* but a more careful consideration will show that they were, in the first instance at any rate, added *to the Lord.* There was formed through faith a vital bond of connection between Him and each penitent and believing soul, in virtue of which that newly-saved one became added to all others who by grace had already believed and become united to the living and exalted Lord. If you are one with Christ, you are one with all who are one with Him. This is the mystical union between Christ and His saints, and between all saints of every church, sect, communion, or fellowship. They may differ in their views of church government, of the nature of the sacraments, of the precise method of inspiration ; they may belong to centuries as far apart as the first from the twentieth ; they may hold high sacramentarian doctrine on the one hand, or be as simple as the Friends or the Salvationists on the other; but so long as there is the least possible union between the soul and Christ, though it be the touch of the garment's hem and the look of the dying malefactor, it is enough to constitute that union in the Holy Catholic Church, the Body of the Risen Lord, the Bride of the King's Son—that new Humanity which Christ is constituting, and which is to supersede every other race throughout the entire world.

Of course, also, as suggested in the analogy of the body, there is one inspiring mind and spirit that communicates unity to the Church. The variety of function and form in the members of the human body is neutralised by the presence and authority of the individual soul. One thought dominates, one purpose presides, one spirit inspires. So is it with the Body of Christ. " There is one Body and one Spirit." " In one Spirit were we all baptized into one body." The Divine Master by His Spirit indwells and governs the entire congregation of faithful souls that belong to Him. Granted that some are paralysed, so that either they do not feel or do not obey His promptings, this does not prevent their being included in the one Body, and some day they will doubtless be vitalised and energised.

The effect of our union in the Body of Christ should be our care for one another. In every individual there is the instinct of self-preservation. If the face is threatened the arm is at once and almost instinctively raised to protect it. If one hand is endangered, the other hand, and indeed the entire body, interposes in a moment to withdraw it and save it. So in Society. When the relations of men to each other are normal, they will stand together for common interests, not class interests, but universal ones—those that affect the well-being of the entire community. Above all, this will be the case with the Church into which the love of God has been shed. Each member of the Church should care for the whole more than for himself, as so to be able to say with the ancient patriot and psalmist : " Let my right hand forget her cunning, let my tongue cleave to the roof of my mouth ; if I prefer not Jerusalem *above my chief joy.*"

The similitude before us compels us to admit the truth of these conclusions. If the analogy of the body holds we can arrive at no other. There is no doubt that the well-being of the whole organism is the common purpose of each subordinate part. Eye, ear, hand, foot

has again and again been freely surrendered
that the body might be preserved. Similarly,
as it was with the early Church, so it should
be in every other, and with the universal
Church most of all. " Not one of them said
that ought of the things which he possessed
was his own."

*The health of the whole reacts upon the
well-being of each.* It might seem that our
Master were asking too much, when He bids
each of us to be willing to sacrifice all that
is dearest and most precious for the common
good. If we reflect for a moment, however,
it becomes evident that He does not ask too
much. When the hand lifts food to the
mouth, is it not contributing to the nourish-
ment of the muscles that control it ? When
the foot bears the body swiftly and surely
to the dining-table, however wearied it may
become, is it not securing for itself the nour-
ishment and sustenance that are absolutely

necessary to its existence ? Similarly, when we are promoting the spiritual health and efficiency of a fellow-believer, we are directly administering, not only to his well-being, and that of the whole Church, but are serving ourselves most substantially.

The way to get daily bread is to say Give *us*; the true path to forgiveness is to say Forgive *us*. In praying for another you pray for yourself. In entreating that some Divine gift may be bestowed upon others you are securing its benefit and comfort for your own soul. " We are members one of another."

VII.

OUR DIVERSIFIED WORK AND GIFTS.

ROM. xii. 6.

THE R.V. reads thus: "*Having gifts differing according to the grace given to us.*" These words are curiously parallel with what the Apostle says of himself, where he defines the source of his authority: "*I say through the grace that was given me*" (ver. 3). The comparison between these two leads Dr. Weymouth in his translation to render our text thus: "WE HAVE SPECIAL GIFTS WHICH DIFFER IN ACCORDANCE WITH THE DIVERSIFIED WORK GRACIOUSLY ENTRUSTED TO US."

It is very gracious of our God and Father to entrust work to us. God Himself is the great

Worker. When He raised the Lord Jesus to His right hand in the heavenlies, He said, " Sit Thou on My right hand, till I make Thine enemies Thy footstool." He must therefore continue to sit there, as enthroned King, till the Father has put all enemies under His feet, and has given the nations for His inheritance, and the uttermost parts of the earth for His possession.

This is the work on which God the Father is now engaged, accomplishing His ends by the Spirit, who proceedeth forth from the Father and the Son to regenerate and transform. The end cometh, but it is not yet, when God shall be all in all. In the interval we are summoned to be workers together with God, so that the people whom we endeavour to influence are God's husbandry, God's building, whilst we are ministers through whom they believe. And thus we plant or we water, but neither is he that planteth anything, nor

he that watereth, but God that uses our poor
work. "Now he that planteth and he that
watereth are one: and every man shall receive
his own reward according to his own labour"
(1 Cor. iii. 8).

This is the true conception of Christian
work. God works all things through us all.
It is with us as with our Lord. We can do
nothing effectively from ourselves. We work
because He works within us by His mighty
and resistless power. The Father abiding in
us doeth His works by and through our
surrendered wills. It was therefore perfectly
right and true that Paul should say that the
things which he wrought for the obedience
of the Gentiles were wrought in and through
him by the power of the Spirit of God.

But is not this high honour, not only that
we should receive the abundance of grace
for our own salvation, but that we should be
summoned to co-operate with God in extending

the knowledge of that grace to others ? Do not say, " Lord, help me," but " Lord, may I help Thee ? " No argument is more potent in producing a holy life than this. Those who work with God must cleanse themselves from all filthiness of the flesh and spirit, and must be so clean in heart and life, that no contagion of evil may mingle with the communication of grace to others. In a hospital once, I saw in the corridor the instruments, to be used in an operation, carried past me in an antiseptic solution.

Not only is it a high honour to co-operate with God, *but it fills us with a great hope.* Supposing that a young disciple, like Raphael, is summoned into the studio of a Michael Angelo, to assist in the production of a masterpiece, at first he is in despair, but as the outlines of the picture are struck out, it becomes clear that ultimate success is certain. The master-brain guarantees it ; those

skilled fingers, in mixing the colours, and
laying on the paint, will secure it ; and so
the neophyte works contentedly and happily
at his little part, satisfied to fill in the assigned
colours, and learning, as he works with the
master, some of his own technique.

But, still further, such co-operation is a
wonderful sedative for the mind and heart.
Under the crushing pressure of trouble, and
amid the world's perplexing cross-lights,
nothing helps us better than to be allowed to
do something, however trivial, for the relief,
guidance, or salvation of others. Many a
crushed heart has slowly come back to life
again from the borders of the grave because
it was compelled to resume some line of
abandoned ministry, in answer to clamant
voices. Our own joy returns, as we make joy
for others. Our own minds perceive the
truth, which we endeavour to explain.

Our work is diversified. Properly so, be-

cause, as we have seen, the needs of the Church
are various. Eyes, ears, hands, feet are all
necessary. One fulfils this function, another
that. But the ultimate decision as to our
place in the body and our service is determined
by the Divine Will. " God hath set the
members every one of them in the body, as
it hath pleased Him." God has set, by His
direct appointment, each of us in the special
place he is called to occupy. Each has a
Divine commission to fulfil, of which he must
render an account to God. Let us not envy or
judge one another. Each stands and falls
to his own master. Let us not depreciate our
own position, nor envy one another, nor be
proud. Our God who doeth after the purpose
of His own will is master of all details. It is
He who appoints some to work in the trenches
at the foundations, and some on the sunlit
height. This man wields the sword and that
the trowel, according to His will : one to be

girded for death amid the stress of some terrible persecution, another to wait for His coming through the slow-moving years. Nebuchadnezzar said truly, "He doeth according to His will in the army of heaven, and among the inhabitants of the earth and none can stay His hand, or say unto Him, What doest Thou?"

Our special gifts vary with our work. We are reminded of the Parable of the Talents, and that the king gave to each according to his several ability. God's gifts are generally closely associated with our natural powers. What is *ability* in the ordinary man becomes a *gift* in the consecrated one. The ability is the channel along which the gift flows. What a man could not do as an ordinary man, becomes augmented after his conversion by that special touch of the Divine Spirit, which refines, purifies, ennobles, and multiplies it, till the raw rock-oil becomes clear, lustrous, and luminous, fit to burn in the palace of royalty.

But we must draw Divine grace into our gifts. The gift is the capsule that waits to be filled by grace. Grace is the free outflow of the Divine nature to man, unbought, unmerited, unearned. It is the issuing forth of the Divine energy to our weakness and need. But we must receive it, use it, reckon on it, be glad and thankful for it. The more we use, the more there is to be used. It is most important to lift up our hearts each time we are called to minister to others, asking that our natural powers may be evidently supplemented by the addition of the Divine helpfulness. The upward look has the power to bring the whole of God's resources to our assistance ; and things can be wrought which we wonder at in all after years.

When Samson started out on his life-career, it is clear that there was nothing in

his outward build to warrant his friends to
expect great feats of strength. The repeated
questions of Delilah, that he would tell her
the secret of his great strength, prove that he
had no special muscular development ; but
he had learnt the art of drawing on the Divine
reservoir. " By faith Samson . . ." The
Spirit of the Lord began to play on him, as
the minstrel on a harp, and he yielded to it,
reckoned on it, and gloried in it. So only can
lions be rent as kids, and gates moved from
their hinges, and the enemies of the Lord
flung heaps upon heaps. So only can the
slightest and least ministry be effectively
performed in Christ's Church.

VIII.

OUR GIFTS—THEIR VARIETY AND USE.

HOW eagerly must each of the servants have opened the scrip that told them how much their master had entrusted them with! The man who had received five felt exhilarated and inspired, as he said to himself, "My master trusts me greatly and expects much of me, and I will not fail him." The man to whom only one talent was given, was startled with the smallness of his opportunity. Perhaps he felt at first that he would make the most of it, though it was so little; but afterwards relapsed into the despair which thought that it was too small to be of any practical use. But the man of the two talents was neither specially elated nor specially depressed, but took his master's gift largely as a matter of course. It did not exalt him or depress. With calm deliberation he went his way to make the best of it. He is the type of the man of average ability, and it is of such that the Apostle is speaking here.

Most of us are just ordinary commonplace people, neither great geniuses nor fools, but entrusted with ordinary talents and opportunities of which we must one day render an account. It has been truly said by Phillips Brooks in this connection : " The average man is by far the most numerous man. The man who goes beyond the average and the man who falls short of the average, both of them, by their very definition, are exceptions. They are the outskirts and fringes, the capes and promontories of humanity. The great continent of human life is made up of average existences, the mass of two-talented capacity and action."

In wealth, there are the extremes of the millionaire and the beggar; but the most, as Agur desired, have neither poverty nor riches. In human experience, some appear to live on sunlit mountains of joy, whilst others spend their days in unbroken sorrow and depression ; but the great mass of men live in the temperate zone, the regions of neither extreme joy nor extreme sorrow, but with a quiet mingling of these elements, one with the other producing a calm and even pathway. So in the Church of God, we have our outstanding Saints, Leaders, Apostles and Prophets, Confessors and Martyrs, but these do not come in the scope of the Apostle's thought. He is dealing with the average Church member, who is possessed of some opportunity and power with which to edify the Church or save the world.

It seems as though the Apostle realised the desirability of stirring up the believers whom he was addressing. He wanted them to give themselves to their ministry, whatever it was, to put diligence into their ruling, cheerfulness into their mercy, liberality into their giving. They were exercising their gifts, but perhaps there were symptoms that they were relaxing the strenuousness and intensity of their first days.

This relaxation is the peculiar temptation of average ability. The exceptional man is conscious that much is expected of him ; that he is always required to do his best, that many eyes are upon him. There is a hush when his face is seen. Men wait for him to speak. But the average man feels nothing of this. He knows that he has never startled men into intense enthusiasm, or plunged them into disappointment and chagrin. He has generally done his day's work without

provoking praise or blame.   He takes himself
for granted, as other men take him for granted.
Why should he exert himself ?   No one expects
him to do a brilliant thing.

There may have been an ambition of that
kind in his heart once, but it has long since
faded away.   He has learnt his limitations.
He can never be John the Beloved any more
than he can be Judas the traitor ; he is just
James, the son of Alphæus or Lebbæus,
whose surname is Thaddeus ; his name will
never occur in the chapters of the Acts of the
Apostles, why should he exert himself to do
anything extraordinary or take special pains !

Has this been your temptation ?   You
may have been living of late on a dead level ;
you have been content with this commonplace routine of mediocrity ; you have not
been exerting your full strength.   But there
is nothing more demoralising to the soul's
best interests than this, and nothing which

will sooner rob you even of such power as you possess.

What, then, is your special gift? Is it *prophecy*, not in the sense of fore-telling, but of forth-telling ? The old word which in the Hebrew tongue was used for prophecy, is akin to our Yeast or East, and to the German *Geist*. It is significant of the sudden uprush of utterance, as of a fountain from a hidden spring It is the true geyser, of which the waters are so hot that they dissolve the ice and snow that cover the surrounding earth, and make an oasis of verdant beauty in the realm of the Frost-King.

The prophet differs from the teacher in that he gives the message of the eternal, whilst the teacher inculcates and enforces that which has been already revealed. Have you the gift of intuitive insight and of appropriate speech ? Take care to proportion your prophecy to your own progress in the

Christian life. Do not go beyond your own experience or obedience. Above all, have respect in your utterances to the foundations of faith which have already been laid.

Is it *ministry*? The word means service of some practical kind. It may include the pastorate or diaconate, the work of the deaconess or the lay-preacher—but whatever it be, let us to whom any sphere of service is entrusted give ourselves to it. It must not be taken up as a by-play or pastime, but must engage the most careful and thoughtful attention of heart and mind. We must toil even to beads of sweat. We must be instant in season and out of season. No stone must be left unturned, no expedient untried, no effort allowed to slacken from express speed to dead-slow.

Is it *teaching*? You must not weary of giving line on line, precept on precept, here a little and there a little. You must sow beside all waters, and on all soils. You must do your work with pains and care, always believing that this or the other pupil may be a Paul, a Chrysostom, or a Paton.

Is it *exhortation* or *consolation*? Is it your province to be like Barnabas, a " son of consolation "? This is one of the most priceless gifts, because the world is full of broken hearts ; but you must be willing to spend much time in patient hearing. Sorrow-stricken souls will no more betray themselves to the hasty and engaged ear than the forest glade will ring with bird-music when boisterous children are shouting in riotous fun. The thorn can only be extracted with careful probing, the wound cannot be dressed without deliberate pains. Be content to treat one case well, rather than to heal lightly the wounds of many sufferers.

Is it *giving*? Has God bestowed on you a sufficiency of income and more, so that there is a margin left for others ?   Be liberal, let your cup run over, use both hands, let the abundance of your joy abound unto the riches of your liberality.   Give whatever you ought to give simply and unaffectedly, re- membering that God is able to make all grace abound towards you.

Are you called to *rule* ?   Some are summoned to stand in the front rank, to be leaders, directors, officials—they must be diligent. A servant whom the Lord hath set over His household, or over any department of it, must be faithful and wise ; he must be awake in the early morning, and watching until the stars, else he will not be able to share out their food to all in due season.

Is your province that of showing *mercy* ? The term probably refers to the visitation of the sick and afflicted—a work requiring a special gift of sympathy that acts as a key to unlock the heart of the sufferer.   See that

you do this with hilarity (this is the literal
rendering of the Greek word). You must go
forth with joyful eagerness, and when you
enter the sick chamber, it must be as when
a shaft of sunlight penetrates through the
cloud.

Thus your two talents will gradually
increase to four—that is, to one short of the
original gift of genius, as represented by the
man of five talents. Better still, you will
be invited one day to enter into the Master's
joy—the joy of His "Well-Done," the joy
of a life well spent and of a work well finished,
the joy of a perfect satisfaction, the joy of
enlargement, the joy of the Father's Bosom.

IX.

THE BLOOM OF MODESTY.

"Abhor that which is evil, cleave to that which is good."
—Rom. xii. 9.

ABHORRENCE is an almost instinctive shrinking from that which excites disgust. It is easier to say and admit this, than to understand why it is that we naturally shrink from some things and are attracted to others. It may be an implanted or an acquired property of the soul, by which it is protected from what would be harmful and destructive, and inclined to what will promote health and well-being. Whether it was originally implanted by the direct act of our Creator, or is the result of the long experience

71

of generations, which has left its indelible
impress on our physical and nervous organisation, we may treasure it as one of the
good gifts which we owe to the Father of
lights.

That the typhoid-breeding drain should
be indicated by the noisome odour, which
forces us to close nose and mouth and turn
to gasp hastily in the fresh air; that vicious
and unnatural actions should offend the eye;
that unwholesome, poisonous food should be
unpleasant to the taste—all these, which are
but specimens of myriads of similar repulsions,
are evidence of the care with which God's
providence helps us to find the path through
the wonderful system of things which we
know as human life. If the reverse had been
the case, and the evil was naturally pleasant
and the good distasteful, we should be compelled to think that malignancy and evil
were seated on the supreme throne.

Of course we must admit that evil things seem more attractive than good to some dispositions ; but that is because their nature, through long use, has become perverted, and they call good evil, and evil good. But these are monstrosities, which contradict that high ideal which God embedded in our constitution when He made us in His image and after His likeness. Children are able, by their very nature, unless heredity or environment has shamefully perverted it, "to know to refuse the evil and choose the good" (Isa. vii. 16).

Let us take care lest by habitual practice, or by our light flirting with evil standards around us, we reach the position in which, instead of abhorring evil and cleaving to the good, we abhor the good and cleave to the evil. "Woe unto them," says the Prophet, "that call evil good, and good evil; that put darkness for light, and light for darkness ; that

put bitter for sweet, and sweet for bitter."
For such, if they should read these words,
there is but one thing to be done, we must
address to them that exhortation of another
Prophet : " Ye who turn judgment to worm-
wood, and cast down judgment to the earth—
seek Him that maketh the Pleiades and Orion,
and turneth the shadow of death into the
morning ! " In other words, they must go
back to their origin ; just as when a ship's
compass has become perverted by the masses
of iron around, it is taken, when on the Clyde,
to some lone loch among the mountains,
that the discrepancy may be remedied.

Take care, whatever you do, not to become
degraded by the low standards of people
around you, so as to lose the acuteness of
your spiritual senses. If you are forfeiting
the delicacy of your pronunciation, get back
to your native city. If you are losing the
quick perceptiveness of the ear, accustom it

for a little to only the finest music. If your
sense of smell is impaired, take a trip into the
mountains of God, inhale their ozone! So
shall you distinguish between things that
differ, and be sincere and void of offence " till
the day of Christ."

The pure heart will instinctively abhor
that which is evil. The unclean allusion,
the polluting page of print or letter-press, the
joke with the double meaning, the suggestion
of the tempter, will make the heart start
backwards, and the blush come on the face.
The path may lie before the feet carpeted
with flowers, but they are the bloom of the
deadly night-shade, the fruit that of the
apples of Sodom ; and the young pure nature
cries with Joseph, " How can I do this great
wickedness ! "

That obvious abhorrence is the witness of
the temper of the heart. The evil-minded
are instantly aware of what is transpiring

beside them. They diagnose the position
instantly. Perhaps that sudden start of
yours reminds them of their own experience
far back in the past. It will probably make
them hate you, as the burglar hates the babe
who is startled by his presence, and cries out.
And as you preserve your sensitiveness to
evil, the Lord will commend you, saying, " I
know thy toil and patience, and that thou
canst not bear evil men, and hast not grown
weary. . . . To him that overcometh to him
will I give to eat of the tree of life, which is
in the Paradise of God."

But the difficulty with many is, how to
preserve that bloom of modesty amid the
blighting atmosphere in which they are
compelled to live, and with that fruit of the
Tree of the Knowledge of Good and Evil of
which we all eat. The secret is here. Remember that you are king in your own soul.
No one can force an entrance unless you

permit. You cannot help the evil, which beats like a sea of ink around the walls; you cannot prevent the noxious fumes of unclean speech or suggestion that float around you; but you can keep doors and windows shut, as you do in the railway-train when passing through a city or neighbourhood where they manufacture chemicals.

You can do better than that. You can burn within your heart sweet spices, or deodorising fragrance that shall keep it pure and sweet, as the Tabernacle of old was kept fragrant by the incense-altar, although the outer court was full of burning sacrifices, that might have made the sacred place offensive. Take the name of Jesus with you; repeat it softly and often to yourself! Let your soul call up its choir of holy thoughts, and let them sing God's high praise. Remember that when all Egypt was wrapped in a darkness that could be felt, Israel had light in their dwellings. There are certain insects which, before they descend into stagnant water, surround and encase themselves in an envelope of oxygen. Learn from them !

But there is yet a further thought. " The fruit of light is in all goodness," says the Apostle (Eph. v. 9, R.V.). Like many of his deepest remarks, it is a parenthesis ; but it is very suggestive. Imagine Light producing fruit. The black soil produces luscious and beautiful fruit, but what must be the texture and taste of the fruit of Light ! But the helpfulness of the thought lies deeper. Fruit comes so easily, so naturally, so gradually ! There is no effort about it. The effort would be evoked by its repression, not by allowing it to mature.

The meaning of the Apostle is here : Deeper than your mind is your heart. See that it is kept open to the Light of God. Let the inner light — the Urim and Thummim

stone on your ephod—be always kept un-
dimmed and clear. When there is the least
dwindling, or blur, or want of focus, stop,
examine into the cause, get right. Come,
ye children, and let us walk in the Light of
the Lord. So shall we be delivered from
the power of darkness, so shall we bear the
fruitage of all goodness, so shall we cleave to
that which is good, and naturally, instinctively
shrink from the first taint of evil.

X.

DILIGENT IN BUSINESS.

Rom. xii. 11.

*B*E *Diligent in Business.* We ought not to take up our daily work as a task which has to be " got through " as quickly as possible, and would not be taken in hand except for the necessity of getting the money-payment which is attached to it. Let every one stop for a moment and ask the question, " What is the inner motive that propels me to my work ? " The majority will reply, " We must earn our living " ; or " We must take up our father's business, and keep it going for the sake of the family " ; or " We want to get settled in life, and there is no way else of procuring a home for the one twin-soul of our choice."

Far be it from me to say that any one of these motives is unworthy or wrong. But it would be a welcome change on these monotonous repetitions to hear one and another putting the matter thus : " We work because we want to add our contribution to the general well-being of the world. We have a solid contribution to make, and we intend to make it as efficiently as possible. Our work is to co-operate, so far as we may, with the great upward movement of the race."

Certain operations must be carried forward or the life of man would become impossible. Food must be brought from the ends of the earth and prepared ; clothes must be made for rich and poor ; there must be light and fuel and driving-power and the means of transit.   Indeed time would fail to complete

6

even the barest enumeration. Divine Providence provides the raw material, but there
is endless service needed to fashion and prepare
it for human use.

Why cannot those who are called to any
branch of human service realise the high
honour it involves, and do what has to be
done heartily, as to the Lord and not to man ?
Was it a more holy work to construct the
ancient Tabernacle, and make clothes for the
sons of Aaron, than to build solid cottages
for our working-people, or make clothes for
the masses of our teeming populations ?

God has summoned each of us to work with
Him in meeting the endless needs of His
great family, and it seems reasonable to assume,
that if once we understood that each of us
is as much called to his occupation—so long
as it is an honourable one—as the pastor is
called to preach, the musician to compose, or
the artist to paint, we should no longer be as

dumb driven cattle, but should leap to our work with alacrity. It is the feeling that we are doing nothing in particular that is so trying to eager and strenuous natures. But the mere cog-wheel is stirred to more accurate and regular rotation when once it realises that it is necessary to the Time-keeping of the City !

" Begone about your business," says a well-known dial in London. Every one should have a business, even though his livelihood is otherwise assured. None are so much to be pitied as the idle rich. Do something, make something, help some one else to produce something. If you have only one talent, invest it with others, that the whole output may repay the great God who has sent you into His world for a purpose.

Don't dawdle ; don't come to your desk or office five minutes late ; and don't begin to prepare for leaving till the hour strikes ;

don't saunter through life ; don't put on
your spurts when your employer's eyes are
upon you, to be succeeded by hours of lethargy
when you fancy yourself unnoticed. Put
your soul into what you do. Take an interest
in it. Read up all information on the business
in which you are engaged, even though your
department is a very humble one. When
you are addressed, answer back cheerfully.
The secret of Budgett's success in Bristol,
years ago, is said to have been that, as a
young man, he performed a difficult task one
morning before breakfast, to the absolute
surprise of the Governor, who thought that
he would spend an entire day over it.

You will never succeed in business unless
you comply with the spirit of the following
conditions :—

(1) You must have definite ideals, not only
of the general course of business-life, but
particularly of your own. Spend time in

thinking how your department might be improved, and how your little niche might be filled more worthily.

(2) Always be on the alert to anticipate the requirements of those above you, and to be even-handed and just to those below. Human machinery is sensitive and delicate to the last degree.

(3) Count no trouble too great to meet the demands of your customers, even though their whims and vagaries appear unreasonable. Deal with them as you would have them deal with you ; and if some one compels you to go a mile with him, go with him twain. Be courteous, obliging, polite, willing to take trouble, giving your brains to those who want your advice and help that they may be saved from mistake.

(4) Distinguish between efficiency and hard work. Of course the latter is always a necessary condition of success, but there are

many who work hard and accomplish little. We need to study the laws of efficiency.

A friend of mine told me recently, that, in remodelling his business, he found that out of seven girl-clerks three were specially gifted with a quick perception, and it was a waste for the firm to keep them toiling at addressing envelopes. They could do better work, and more of it, if they were set to deal with the correspondence. We should see to work being done by those who are adapted to meet its special demands ; and not employ razors to cut blocks !

The selection of work-people and their assignment to the special tasks for which they are adapted by nature and training, is of incomparable importance in a successful business career ; and in dealing with men, it must ever be a guiding principle that to show how work should be done is never to waste time. Better to teach one man to help you, than to do the work of a dozen men. He will make the greatest success who does least himself, but knows how to avail himself of the help of others.

To get the most out of another, remember not to scold when he does wrong; but encourage and praise whenever you have the least reason for doing so. Speak encouragingly to your subordinates. A cheery word will often help a horse over a steep bit of road, while all the flogging you could administer would fail. It is good " to impute righteousness," if we may put it so. Is not this the manner in which God elicits the best from us ? Christ says to one of His servants : " You are Simon Bar-Jonas, the son of a timid dove, but you are capable of becoming Peter, a Rock-man." Immediately that disciple seeks to justify the Master's anticipations.

If any one shall live thus, towards his superiors, his inferiors, and his customers, it

is almost impossible that he should not get
on, especially if his living-expenses are kept
within a narrow competence for the first few
years. But even if not, there will be a sense
of pleasure, of interest, of zest, which will
transform drudgery into delight, and make the
workshop or store a very temple in which
service shall be rendered such as will refresh
the heart of God.

Because we serve the Lord Christ, whatever
we do, we are to do it unto Him. Six days
thou shalt labour! Man goes forth to his
labour till the evening! Therefore what thy
hand finds to do, do it with thy might, and the
days will be filled with the music of something
accomplished, something done.

XI.

THE THREE-FOLD CORD—DILIGENT, FERVENT, DEVOUT.

Rom. xii. 11.

WE have already seen a little of what is included in the Apostle's injunction, "Be diligent in Business." But there is nothing in legitimate business life that should, or need, conflict with fervour.

The fervent spirit is one in which a hidden fire is burning, like that in the Tabernacle of old, the seat of which was the Propitiatory— the golden slab that covered the Ark. When God has once kindled that fire in your heart, see that it never goes out, but is constantly supplied with the fuel of truth, maintained in

an atmosphere of Faith and Prayer. To read
the Bible is not enough : we must find time in
the early morning to meditate on it, until the
Scriptures become shot through with the
Heavenly Light, as clouds suffused and saturated by the level beams of the setting or rising
sun.

Keble sings of those who, as they tread the
crowded street or wrangling mart, repeat the
melody of some sweet secret strain ; and it is
surely not impossible to do so, if we are attuned
to Heaven's minstrelsy, before we enter on
our day's programme, and if, from time to
time, the soul casts an upward glance to the
face of Christ. " My heart is bubbling over
with good matter," said the Psalmist, who, in
making things concerning the King, had
learnt the Divine secret of the burning heart.

A business man told me that, whenever he
lost the sense of the Presence of Christ, he
would retire into his private room, kneel down

and address the Spirit of God in this manner :
" Holy Spirit, what have I done, in that Thou
hast withdrawn from me the sense of the
Presence of my Lord ? "   He said that almost
instantly he was reminded of some point in
which he had refused the Spirit's leading or
warning, and as soon as this was adjusted the
light broke in again upon him.

The habit, also, of ejaculatory prayer is
very salutary ; and many a time, instead of
treating a customer or traveller to some kind
of bait, the salesman would ask, that if it
were possible, such and such a transaction
should be carried through, it would be a
matter of constant astonishment and of infinite
pleasure to see how the blessing of the Lord
was prospering and giving good success,
without a tinge of added sorrow.

But the solvent of all perplexity is to
understand the true conception of life, con-
tained in that significant phrase, *serving the*

Lord. The Greek really means, " being en-
slaved to the Lord."

It is so impossible for us to realise what
slavery meant and means. The absolute
proprietorship of the master blotted out the
right of choice, dissolved the bonds of marriage,
made wife and children the chattels of the
owner, like the young of the fold or pen.
The slave-girl who bungled her lady's locks
in preparing her for the festival might be
branded by the hot iron, if it suited her lady's
whim. The slave-boy whose bended back
quivered under the draught-board placed on it,
so as to disarrange the pieces, might be flung
into his master's lamprey-pond to feed the
fish. No judge or court could interpose to
arraign the master or mistress who vented
tempestuous passion on their long-suffering
property.

But this was the favourite word of which
the Apostles made perpetual use. This

Apostle begins his greatest treatise by intro-
ducing himself as the slave of Jesus Christ.
This was a higher rank in his estimation than
to be the scholar of Gamaliel, or a citizen of
Rome. Peter, also, speaks of those who
denied the Lord that bought his readers
to be His own, and reminds them that their
price was neither gold nor silver, but precious
blood. This also led to that allusion to the
brand-marks of Jesus, which proves that
the wounds and bruises of the saints were
viewed with pride, as having scored them to be
the inalienable property of the Heavenly
Master.

Why should not this same conception be
the guiding and moulding principle of our own
lives? Why should we not feel that we have
been allocated by the direct arrangement of
Christ to our several tasks? He distributes
talents according to our natural abilities; and
if he does this, He must surely determine also

where those talents are to be expended !
The one involves the other.

George Herbert speaks of the Oriental
fragrancy of those sweet words, " My Master
Jesus "; and however distasteful our task
may be, surely the fact that it is being performed for Him makes our fingers drop with
spices, even when we lift the iron latch of the
door of daily toil. The Master has been there
before us, and has satisfied Himself that there
are reasons why we should be located in that
very spot—perhaps that we may learn to
bear the yoke in our youth, or help some
fainting soul to endure.

When, in the olden time, an Israelite was
hard pressed by poverty, he might make over
his service, for seven years at least, to some
neighbouring landowner. Leaving his little
cottage and patch of ancestral property, he
would carry his wife and children over to
the big mansion with its adjacent buildings,

where they would be provided for during the immediate crisis, and until brighter heavens smiled on them. It was an admirable intermediate arrangement. But when the difficult time was overpast, the peasant proprietor, unwilling to face again the hardships and privations of the past, might come to his protector and say, " I would rather stay with you, than adventure my craft on the troubled waters." In that case, the public officials would be summoned, and, in their presence, the man's ear was bored to the door-post of his master's house, as he repeated the formula, " I love my master, and will not go out free." It was slavery, but such slavery has brought with it an immense relief from debt, anxiety, robbers, Arab tribes, prepared at harvest and vintage to swoop down on the hardly-raised crops (Ex. xxi. 1–10).

In the 40th Psalm and the 52nd chapter of Isaiah this ancient custom is referred to when our Lord is described as the obedient Servant whose ears have been bored to the door of His Father's will. Such is the peace which accrues to the heart which has chosen the Mastership of Jesus; and asks that henceforth none should trouble it, since there could be no rivalry, no division of interest, and no scattered service.

Why, we ask it again, why should not this parable of Christian enslavement be ours? We have looked this way and that. Other masters than Christ have had dominion over us. Our eye has not been single and our mind has been darkened. We have served Christ fitfully, and with now flowing and now ebbing tides. But the end of this separate ownership has surely arrived. Let us *now* transfer ourselves and all that belongs to us to the Divine Redeemer, giving Him the inventory of our goods and the title-deeds of our estate; and asking Him henceforth to be responsible for us and ours ; whilst, on our part, we promise to be only for Him and His.

Whether we live let us live unto the Lord ; and as a tiny silk ball, by repeatedly striking a bar of iron, suspended horizontally, will make it move with ever-increasing velocity, so as daily we repeat the words, " My Master, this is for Thee," life will receive a new and blessed impulse Christwards from every incident.

XII.

THE LIMITS OF SELF-DEPRECIATION.

" In honour preferring one another."—Rom. xii. 10.

IT is not difficult to do this when we really
love. The most natural thing for
any lover is to put the loved one forward,
and to find the truest pleasure in knowing
that his choice has been ratified and endorsed
by the unanimous feeling of those whose
opinion counts. When the Apostle, therefore,
bids us be kindly affectioned one to another
in brotherly love, it follows as a necessary
consequence that he should add, " in honour
preferring one another." For a mother to see
her son's hard labours crowned by the aca-
demic degree, or the well-deserved appoint-

ment to some high office, is to fill her cup to
the full with the blessedness of unselfish
gladness.

Also, when our love is not quite so close and
strong, it is always wiser to stand aside, where
honours are being showered around, and let
others get them if they will.   To seek honour
for yourself is to forfeit your self-respect and
all right to it.   If it comes to us naturally
and rightfully, we should certainly take it,
because it gives us a stronger power towards
helping and blessing the world.   But never
grasp at it for its own sake.   Remember
the Master's words : " How can ye believe,
which receive honour one of another, and seek
not the honour that cometh from God only ? "

Do not we all need a baptism of love that
we shall take a generous and unselfish pleasure
when the worth of another is recognised ?
Chrysostom says, " When the head is crowned
the feet strut."   Sometimes jealousy in its

incipient stages may be arrested by a very strenuous and resolute effort on our part to secure the right understanding and honouring of some one with whom we have had variance of feeling, some slight ruffling on the surface of the inner lake. If your friend or rival really deserves honour, be sure to accord it. Don't stint your praise. It is for this reason that one loves the great social games like football and base-ball, in which the player does not think exclusively of his own stroke, but loses himself in his team or side. It is good to hear the shout across the field, " Well played ! " and to join in the enthusiasm with which the victor is greeted by his side, as he leaves the field, though not one of them has gained a score of which he can possibly be proud. More of the same spirit in Christian life would be very acceptable. None for himself, but all for Jesus Christ ! There is a profound lesson to be learnt from the habit

of Eastern literary men, of whom it is said
that often it is necessary to read half through
a book before you arrive at such a sentence
as this, indicating the authorship : " Such is
the humble opinion of the writer, who is not
worthy to remove the dust from the feet of
the reader—Selim of Mecca."

And to those who live thus, there will come
quite naturally and beautifully all the honour
they can bear. We must never seek honour
as the goal of our life's ambition. To do our
life-work as nobly and strenuously as possible
must be our destined end and aim ; and that
will, of itself, always bring, in well-constituted
societies, honour in its train. But there is a
whole heaven of difference between this and
that looking round every corner for the opportunity of an advertisement, elated if it is
given, but depressed and spiritless if withheld.
In this also our Lord's words are fulfilled,
" He that loveth his life shall lose it, and he

who hates finds it." Promotion cometh
neither from the East nor West, but from God.
He setteth up one, and putteth down another.
It is for Him to say by what agents He will
do His work in the world; and whilst Haman
thinks that the Kingdom exists for him, if
God desires to honour Mordecai, He will carry
His purpose through by Haman's own hands,
and will ultimately entrust His humble servant with the keys of the Kingdom. Read
again those jubilant outbursts of amazed and
adoring congratulation sung by Hannah,
Elizabeth, and the Mother of our Lord.

Those who are sure that God will honour
them, so far as is good and by such methods
as He may devise, may witness without
jealousy the honouring of fellow-workers,
and with full-hearted joy may assist in the
acknowledgment of their deserts.

But while we live in the success and recogni-
tion of others, we must beware of allowing

ourselves to fall into a habit of self-deprecia-
tion, which is always standing back from
responsibility and duty. We may be so
sensitive to our failures, and so depreciate
ourselves, as to fail to give adequate expression
to the idea which God has incarnated in our
constitution. We have no right to *kow-tow*
to a man who is unworthy ; we have no right
to yield to another a function which the
Master has evidently assigned to us, and for
the exercise of which we must one day hand
in our account. You may be quite willing
to give all honour to another, but you must not
surrender to incompetent hands an office
which you have been sent to fulfil. Do not
think too highly or too meanly of yourself ;
but think soberly, and remember that it is
by the grace of God that you are what you
are.

Many are withheld from getting the most
out of life, and from giving pleasure to those

who love them, because they under-estimate
their capacities, but as we step out in faith
we shall find that as the day is so will the
strength become, and we shall be able to do
all things through Christ that strengtheneth.

Many attitudinise in the looking-glass of
public favour, not as it really is, but as they
conceive it to be, until they rob themselves
of all spontaneity and ease.   They are always
questioning what people think or say, instead
of going forward to be just their simple, easy,
natural selves.   Be quite willing to give all
praise to others, and prefer them to all the
honour they deserve, but do not hesitate to
be yourself, and live your life, and shine for
the Master in the small sphere which He has
selected for you.   And when each day is
done, get into His presence, look up to Him,
and be content if He is pleased ; then ask
Him to go over the mistakes of the day,
smoothing out the creases, straightening the

crookednesses, untying the tangles you may
have caused.

There is nothing more important for us all
than to be absolutely natural, and if the
temptation comes for the introspective, sensitive, and shy disposition to reveal itself, do
two things. First, look up to God to live His
life through you ; and secondly, look around
to see some sign, some lonely soul, some opportunity which will show you what you may do
or say. Above all, love is the solvent, and it is
by the liberal use of this golden key that most
of our perplexities will open their portals,
and admit into rooms of happy ministry.
Love is self-forgetting. Beneath its im-
perious force, the most nervous will tell their
secret to the one whom they adore, and the
most lethargic will shake off their sloth.
There is no restraint or constraint that love
will not trample to atoms under its hastening
feet. The unripest fruit will ripen beneath

its burning sunshine, and the latest flower
will unfold its petals. Then neither encour-
aged by our desire for honour or reward, nor
deterred by the fear of slight and rebuff, we
shall press on to do the task which stands in
front of us, for God's sake and for the world.
Prefer one another, if honour is to be awarded ;
but where duty or danger calls, act as though
the entire weight of reponsibility must be
discharged by you alone. The Master calls
to serve, to wounds and stripes, to hard and
irksome toil. Do you not hear His ringing
voice, sounding through the din of the world's
clamour : "If any man serve Me, let him
follow Me ; and where I am, there shall also
My servant be : if any man serve Me, him will
My Father honour"? And when God honours,
there are awards enough within His bestowal
to satisfy the expectation of every faithful
servant to the uttermost.

XIII.

THE ABOUNDING LIFE.

Rom. xii. 12–13.

ONE is sorely tempted to devote a chapter
to each of the five following clauses, but
in doing so, it would not be possible to set
out the full-orbed beauty of a holy (*i.e.* a
whole) life,—one which is able to meet each
phase or experience, as it comes, with its
appropriate temper. Some dispositions are
strong in one direction, but lacking and de-
ficient in another. They resemble wind-
driven trees. But the noblest lives are sym-
metrical in their development, and without
effort adapt themselves to each demand of
their environment. They are like well-built

boats, which live equally well in any sea.
There is in some Christians an exuberance
of all-conquering life, which is almost greedy
of new experiences, because so sure that they
can do all things through Him that strengtheneth them.   In all things they are more
than conquerors through Him who loves
them.

Five different demands are perpetually
recurring in our lives, and the Apostle sets
himself to indicate how we should comport
ourselves in each of these.   They are the
protracted discipline of life, the pressure of
trouble, the delay in answers to prayer, the
demands made on us by other lives, whether
of our own circle or of strangers.   In each
of these we are taught our appropriate duty.
With his exact command of language the
Apostle strikes out the precise attitude we are
to adopt and the spirit to evince.

In the protracted discipline of life—Rejoice

in Hope. Hope, as depicted by Mr. Watts, is represented as sitting on the rapidly-revolving earth, with downcast head and blinded eyes, unable to discern that the morning star is in the sky, but pressing to her ear the last string of a broken lyre, which she thrums. The Apostle takes off the blindfold, bids her look up and descry the herald rays of the coming dawn. He makes her face radiant with the smile of glad anticipation. He causes her to sing to her lyre, " In Hope, rejoicing."

The emblem of the anchor cannot, after all, be superseded. The ship is still exposed to the billows, that race in one after another from the ocean, but already its anchor has been carried into the haven, and lodged securely there. The rope is strong, and as it is being slowly wound around the capstan, at every turn the distance is lessened, and the ship approaches the still water immediately in view. What a relief to the wave-washed

crew when they feel the pull of the shore.
They are no longer exposed to the fluctuations
of hope and fear.   They count on the shore as
already won ;   and the voyage is as good as
done.   So the believer, who has learnt to
reckon on God, counts the unseen as equally
real with the seen, and the distant as entering
into his calculations equally with the near.
The native of the valley of Chamonix has a
vast advantage over the visitor of a week's
duration, because the latter may never see
the monarch of the mountains on account
of the prevailing clouds and mists, but the
native has become accustomed to reckon on
its presence equally when unveiled as veiled.
Thus hope already enjoys the unseen things
which are as real as the seen, though she has
no security for them other than that provided
by faith.   Faith says that there is a promised
land, and Hope already feeds on its fruit.
Faith brings with her the title-deeds, but

Hope enters on the possession.   Thus we are
to rejoice in our abounding hope.

Under the pressure of trouble—Be patient.
The Greek word is *remaining under*.   What can
a child of God do else ?   He believes that all
things are ordered by the Divine governance,
and hesitates to evade or escape from the
discipline, which may be needed.   Of course
we have a right to seek deliverance from anything which is unnatural or unmerited, as
when our Lord evaded the wrath of His
enemies, and bade His persecuted saints flee
from one city to another to avoid their foes.
We may remonstrate with our foes, as our
Lord did in the hall of Caiaphas.   But when
an overwhelming conjunction of affairs takes
place, which cannot be avoided, and which
befalls us because we persist in well-doing
and in the way of Righteousness, there is
nothing to be done but quietly remain under
our heavy sorrows until the Father says,

" It is enough." It is thus that David bore himself—though he drank a cup which his sin had mixed — under the avalanche of sorrow, which befell him at the hands of Absalom. "And the king said, carry back the ark of God into the city : if I shall find favour in the eyes of the Lord, He will bring me again, and show me both it and His habitation ; but if He say thus, I have no delight in thee ; behold, here am I, let Him do unto me as seemeth good unto Him." If by the use of means you see your way to escape your persecutors, you are at liberty to take it, so far as God enables you ; but if not, be still and wait the Lord's leisure. He will incline unto you and deliver you. It is good for a man to hope and quietly wait for the salvation of the Lord. But let all the hours of waiting be filled with a quiet ministry to others in similar and sadder circumstances, and under the mild radiance of an indefinable dignity and grace. This is what the Apostle John called " the patience of Jesus," and is closely allied to His kingdom. In fact the two are one, because when that patience comes to the soul, it has already had its coronation (Rev. i. 9).

In delayed answers to prayer—Be earnest and persistent. If the Syrophœnician woman had gone home after the first apparent refusal that she received, she would not have found the demon exorcised, and her child lying on the bed. God often seems to deny, or at least be reluctant, that He may teach us lessons in the art of prayer, and lead us on to positions which we had never supposed possible. The soul that is acquiring these lessons emulates the courage with which Moses espoused the cause of his people, and, so to speak, championed it amid the brooding clouds of Sinai. He thought that he was inducing God to have mercy, whereas God was inducing

him to advance to conceptions of His long-
suffering, which led to the vision of the rear-
guard glory of the Divine procession and to the
transfiguring of his own face. " What makes
Mother's face so beautiful ? " said a wild young
officer to his sister. " It is because she spends
so much time in praying for you," she replied.
Go on praying, though the time seems long;
where you kneel now to intercede, you will
presently kneel with adoring gratitude to give
thanks. Only be sure that you are in the
line of God's purpose, then continue instant
in prayer.

*There are, lastly, the demands made by the
necessities of the saints, and by the needs of
those who " for the sake of the Name " have gone
forth taking nothing of the Gentiles.—In regard
to each of these, show large-hearted generosity.*
Paul went to incredible exertion, in minister-
ing to the saints (Rom. xv. 25). He specially
commended those who set themselves to

this service (1 Cor. xvi. 15).   John the Beloved
did the same (3 John 5-8).   The Mosaic
Law enjoined the same holy duty (Lev. xxv.
35-46).   Hospitality is distinctly a Christian
grace (Heb. xiii. 1-3).   The life in which God's
life is enshrined is always giving forth in
ministry, or receiving weary and helpless
creatures into the capacious hostelry of its
Love.   For there are many ways of ministry,
as there are necessities other than those for
physical supplies ; and the big heart of love
is a sheltering caravanserai in which there
is always room for Joseph and Mary and the
Babe Christ.

XIV.

ALL SORTS AND CONDITIONS OF MEN.

ROM. xii. 13–16.

IN the morning you leave your room, where you have seen the Face of God, and renewed your living contact with Realities, and come down into the world, where, as the Psalmist says, " Every man walketh in a vain show, surely they are disquieted in vain." We realise thankfully that this is not our home, but that we are strangers and pilgrims in this transitory time-sphere, as were all our fathers. At the same time we are called to encounter all sorts and conditions of men, as varied in dress, and speech, and attitude towards us, as the crowds that Shakespeare puts upon the stage. As we step out, we utter two sentences, one to ourselves and the other to God. To ourselves we say : " I will take heed to my ways that I sin not with my tongue ; I will keep my tongue with a bridle, while the wicked is before me " ; and to God we say : " And now, Lord, what wait I for ? My hope is in Thee. Deliver me from all my transgressions : Make me not the reproach of the foolish."

Now, let us see how the Apostle would have us bear ourselves in the midst of this motley moving crowd, whom we encounter in the public conveyance, the office, the store, the market-place.

Here among the first is a virulent and persistent *persecutor* of that which is good. We never meet him but he has a snarl against Religion, or some sharp and bitter taunt for us. We know what is coming, and prepare to meet it, not with silence, or averted face,

or scorn for scorn. We remember what the
Psalmist said, as quoted by Peter (i Pet. iii. 9),
and what Paul says here. We love life and
would see many days ; we remember that our
Father sends His sun and rain on the fields of
the churl ; we therefore meet the man with a
smile, a kindly greeting, and a blessing. He
goes away confounded. His shots are received in soft sand and buried there. What
is the good of reviling, where an equable
temper laughs good-naturedly at his words,
and devises some kindly method of reply ?
" If ye are called to suffer for righteousness'
sake, blessed are ye ; and fear not their
fear, neither be troubled ; but sanctify in
your hearts Christ as Lord." " If ye are
reproached for the Name of Christ, happy are
ye, for the Spirit of glory and of God resteth
upon you." " This shall turn to my salvation, through the supply of the Spirit of
Jesus Christ."

So from this encounter you pass on with a happy heart, and within a few steps you meet some *rejoicing individual*, whose cup is flowing over. He is on his way to his wedding; or he has made a discovery which is likely to shed riches into his lap, or a little child has been born in the night, or he has won a prize, or he has entered into the life of God. He stops you on the street to tell you all about it. You feel that you dare not hasten the disclosure that he desires to make, lest you should betray the least indifference, and so you linger, with warm congratulations, in which there is no tinge of jealousy or envy. You enter into his joy; you make him feel that you, as elder brother, need no entreaty to come into the midst of his merry-making, with the music and dancing of Luke xv.

You have hardly left your happy friend, when you meet another, who is almost in tears. He is *a man of sorrowful spirit*, who

just now is passing through the valley of
Baca.   The sorrows of his heart are enlarged.
He has had bad news from his son in Australia,
or his wife is very ill and there is no one to
care for his children, or he has received notice
to leave the situation which he thought was
a permanency, or the office in which he
invested his life's savings has failed. You
cannot tear yourself away from him. He is
quick to notice whether you are in a hurry,
as every one else seems to be. He must be
deliberate, that you may fully understand
and sympathise. He wants to explain the
aggravations, which make his an uncommon
case of woe. You listen, you sympathise,
you take his hand in yours, you dare not
urge him to look on the brighter side ; you
will do that when you call on him in the evening, or on the following day ; but now, it
is best to let the full cisterns of his grief
exhaust themselves, so you just weep with

this man who weeps. " When Jesus saw her
weeping, and the Jews also weeping which
came with her, He groaned in the spirit, and
was troubled, and said, Where have ye laid
him ? They say unto Him, Lord, come and
see. Jesus wept."

Leaving your sad friend, you encounter
next a man *with whom you differ* in tempera-
ment, in his political views, in his attitude
towards social and ecclesiastical questions.
There is hardly a point of contact between
you, except that he is undoubtedly a true
Christian. He is Radical, and you Con-
servative ; he is a Democrat, and you a
Republican ; he is an Episcopalian, and you a
Methodist ; he is inclined to Mysticism, and
you to Pragmatism. But there is this point
of contact, that you are one in Christ, members
of His Body, of His Flesh and Bone. By
mutual agreement you meet on that common
ground, and you are " of the same mind one

toward another." Though temperamentally
you are as different as Euodias and Syntyche,
you are of the same mind in the Lord. You
meditate on the same Scriptures, you have
the same hope, you are subject to the same
God of patience and comfort, and it is not
difficult, therefore, to be of one accord and
one mind. Islands may bear different fruits,
and be of different configuration, but they
are probably spurs of the same uniting
mountain-range (Rom. xv. 4, 5 ; Phil. ii. 2 ;
and iv. 2).

These have been men of your own standing,
but, within a few yards, you encounter *a
man of low estate.* When you see him in the
distance, you make up your mind to pass
him. The pavement is full of fashionably-
dressed folk, with whom you are anxious to
stand well. In the roadway, elegant carriages
and expensive automobiles are glancing past.
Rank, wealth, beauty are in evidence. You

met them last night, you may meet them
again. These people would surely misinter-
pret you if you were to be seen in conversa-
tion with some humble member of your Church.
But you refuse to entertain the suggestion;
you remember that what is highly esteemed
among men is abomination in the sight of
God; that every valley shall be exalted,
whilst every high thing shall be made low;
you recall the Apostle's exhortation to have
the mind of Christ, who though He was rich
became poor, and humbled Himself to become
obedient to the death of the Cross. You
arrest your steps; you recognise that you are
in the presence of one of the sons or daughters
of God; you associate freely with one of your
humbler brethren to your greater enrichment,
and to his comfort.

And presently leaving all these, you turn
to God to ask that you may never be " wise
in your own conceit." One of the most

exquisite of all the Psalms is that which was probably in our Lord's heart, when He spoke the marvellous words of Matt. xi. 25. "Lord, my heart is not haughty, nor mine eyes lofty; neither do I exercise myself in great matters or in things too wonderful for me. Surely I have stilled and quieted my soul; my soul is with me like a weaned child." And in answer, Christ will bring every thought into subjection to His obedience, and make and keep you as a little child (Psa. cxxx.; 2 Cor. x. 5).

XV.

OUR ENEMIES AND HOW TO
SERVE THEM.

ROM. xii. 17–21.

IN the Septuagint version of Proverbs iii.
3, which the Apostle quotes here, we
are bidden to bind Mercy and Truth around
our neck and write them, as though for
constant reference, on the tablet of our heart.
This will secure for us favour and good
understanding in the sight of God and man.
If we order our lives on these two great principles, we shall do all that lies in our power
to live peaceably with all the world. Of
course the world, for these very reasons, will
not live peaceably with us. It has been the

experience of all the saints, who have sought
to embody Mercy and Truth in life and speech,
that in the world they have had perpetual
tribulation, but this has given them con-
siderable satisfaction, for it has proved that
they were not of the world, or the world would
have loved its own ; and they have realised
that they were pilgrims and strangers on the
earth.

When the good king Jehoshaphat, entangled
in an evil alliance, and uneasy with the un-
animity of the false prophets, asked Ahab
whether there were not a prophet of Jehovah
at hand, that they might inquire of him, the
king of Israel replied : " There is yet one
man by whom we may inquire of the Lord,
Micaiah the son of Imlah, but I hate him, for
he doth not prophesy good concerning me but
evil." And similar testimony has been borne
in every age by the servants of the Lord.
" Woe is me, my mother," cried Jeremiah,

" that thou hast borne me a man of strife and a man of contention to the whole earth ! I have not lent on usury, neither have men lent to me on usury ; yet every one of them doth curse me."

We must not be provocative : nor must we give men reasonable grounds for disliking us because of our behaviour towards them or our personal peculiarities. Probably George Fox exposed himself to a large amount of needless dislike, because of his insistence on wearing his hat in the presence of the magistrates of his time. But when conscience is concerned, there can be no parleying or hesitancy ; our course lies straight before us, and we must take the way of the Cross. Under such circumstances we must pay no man evil for evil, but contrariwise blessing.

It is the most natural thing in the world to feel indignant and resentful, when evil things are being said and done. Indignation is

probably akin to righteous anger, because it
realises the moral blackness of some high-
handed wrong; but it is very difficult to be
angry and not to sin, because we are so prone
to pass from the deed to the person who has
perpetrated it, and to feel on fire to avenge
ourselves. This is resentment. Even if we
dare not, or do not show it, this virus is apt
to colour the whole attitude of our thoughts
and feelings, turning them to vinegar and
gall.

It is against this temper of the soul that the
Apostle sets himself. "Avenge not yourselves," he says, " but rather give place unto
wrath." This may mean, Do not oppose a
man's passion, but give it room to expend
itself, like a whirlwind in an open country.
Those who have had to deal with barking
dogs will generally agree that if you walk on
and take no notice, they will get tired and
subside, but if you turn round and fight them,

you will increase their fury beyond bounds.
So with angry men, their wrath burns out like
a fire in crackling thorns, unless you begin to
fight them with their own weapons, then they
that take the sword perish by the sword.   Or
the words may mean, " Leave room for the
anger of God that He may punish ; for it is
written, Revenge is Mine : I will pay back,
saith the Lord."   Probably the latter is the
truer rendering, and it includes the former.
The one thing to be sure of is that you are
hated, not for yourself or anything that you
have done, but because you are a representative and child of the Light.   If this is
so, then the wrong done you is a matter for
your Heavenly Father to deal with.   When
an ambassador to a foreign court receives a
slight, he may realise keenly the injustice
and indignity that have been shown him, but
he does not seek to exact reparation for himself or by the threat of personal vengeance.

The matter is one for his Sovereign and Nation to deal with. He steps aside from the fray, and acts on his instructions. So the child of God acts, not anxious to see his enemies suffer, but to see the Truth vindicated, that the humble may hear and be glad, and that iniquity may shut her mouth. This is the spirit which inspires so many of the Psalms, as for instance, " Help us, O God of our Salvation, for the glory of Thy Name : Wherefore should the heathen say, Where is their God ? Let the revenging of the blood of Thy servants which is shed be known among the heathen in our sight " (Ps. lxxix 9, 10).

Thus the heart is at leisure from its wrath and resentment. The matter is handed over to God, who is a God that judges in the earth, and it is most remarkable to notice how inexorable and inevitable the divine judgments are. Do you not remember the ancient example of this in Judges i. 6, 7 ? " Adoni-bezek fled; and they pursued after him, and caught him, and cut off his thumbs and his great toes. And Adoni-bezek said, Threescore and ten kings, having their thumbs and their great toes cut off, gathered their meat under my table; as I have done, so God hath requited me."

The only time when we are justified in resisting wrong is when some woman, child, or weakling is concerned. It is part of our Christian duty to stand in the front of them, as our Lord did in the hour of His arrest, when He stood between the servants of the high priest and His disciples, and gave them time and opportunity to escape. But even then our interposition will probably be rather in the form of remonstrance, than of the use of force. The main thing for us is not to get angry for ourselves, but to stand calmly and humbly in the strength of God, sure that they who are with us are more than those against us, and that Jehovah rideth on the heavens to our help.

When the heart is right with God, it looks out on men and their doings with an infinite pity, as Jesus did when Malchus' ear had been struck by Peter's sword, and He asked His captors to slacken the binding cords—" Suffer ye thus far "—in order that He might reach forth His hand and touch it ; or as when, on being lifted to the Cross, He began to pray for those who crucified Him, not knowing what they did.   It is thus that we are able to feed our enemy's hunger and quench his thirst. In China, an old Chinaman, who had been the catechist of W. C. Burns, told me that on one occasion, when robbers had stripped him of all his belongings and were going off with them, he called them back to explain how to use his various instruments, his razor, and to wind his watch, etc.   " You are bad sons," he said, " to take my things, but at least you may as well learn how to use them." They were so touched with this, and his prayer for them, that they returned all.

There is no better way· of quelling resentment and ill-feeling in our breast than by doing *kind* things to those who have injured us. We cannot begin by loving with all our *heart*, but we can love with our *strength*. Light one jet of your nature, and the fire will spread to the others. As you act right, speak right, and pray right, you will come finally to feel right ; and instead of being overcome of evil, evil will only evoke and establish the quality of selfless goodness.

XVI.

OUR ATTITUDE TO GOVERNMENT.

" Render to all their dues."—Rom. xiii. 7.

PAUL was a Roman citizen, and when writing to Rome, he does not hesitate to extol the great system of law, order and statecraft for which Rome stood. To the creative genius of the Greek we owe poetry, architecture, sculpture, and philosophy,—all that contributes to the joy of life. To the Roman, on the other hand, we owe the conception of the State, the rights of property, and the sanctity of the home. From the beginning of time—it has been said recently— the races of Aryan extraction were deeply imbued with the conviction of the importance of law, but it was reserved for the Romans to develop that instinct. With them the State was based on the sacrifice of individual rights and the delegation of personal power for the common weal. Self was laid on one side—the good of the community was everything. Cæsar was thus the representative of the common purpose, the embodiment of the national ideal. That individual emperors fell far beneath that ideal, and failed to realise that purpose, was indubitable; and Paul recognised this, when in evident allusion to Nero, he said, "I was delivered out of the mouth of the lion."

The result of Rome's influence in the world was to give stability to human society. The Greek made life beautiful, the Roman made it secure. It is a remarkable fact that these two streams of influence are still flowing strongly through the world. Since the Renaissance, the Greek has led our thought and cultivated our taste, while the Roman ideal of Government still underpins our whole system of jurisprudence. We are still taught that there must be the surrender of general idiosyncracies on the one hand, and on the other the protection of private rights. " The laws of Solon, of Lycurgus and others have withered and died ; but the laws of Rome remain, a stately and fruit-bearing tree, under whose wholesome shade the civilisation of Europe has sprung up and flourished."

We can hardly wonder, therefore, that when the Apostle looked at this mighty organisation, which kept the barbarians at bay, which established everywhere through the world of that time the Roman law, the Roman officials, and the Roman peace, he spoke of it in the eulogistic terms of this paragraph. Patriotism is the legitimate child of Religion. Was there ever a keener patriot than Isaiah or Jeremiah ? Was it not of the essence of patriotism, when our Lord wept over Jerusalem, as He anticipated the gathering of the eagles over the lifeless carcase of His people ? Have not the great saints of the Church, men like Bernard or Luther or Knox, been devoted patriots ? " Lives there a man with soul so dead, that never to himself has said, This is my own, my native land ? " Cherish patriotism as part of your religion, although you realise that your citizenship is in Heaven, and that your true country lies in the eternal. In Christ there is neither Jew nor Greek, barbarian nor Scythian—therefore you discard your national antipathies and animosities ; and when they are laid aside, the flame of true patriotism will burn the brighter. On the whole, then, we are bound by the decisions of the Government under which we elect to live, subjecting our personal preferences and tastes to the general conclusions to which our Nation may be led.

There is one notable exception, however.
As long as we accept the protection given us
by Cæsar, we are bound to give Cæsar his
penny. "Render unto Cæsar the things that
are Cæsar's," said our Lord. But when Cæsar
goes beyond his province, and demands things
which are not his, but God's, then another
principle steps in, and we are bound to refuse
to give to the earthly ruler that to which he
has no right, however vociferously he claim
it. What are these things of God? Obviously
our conscience, our loyalty to the Divine
voice, our devotion to the Divine order.

So long as Nebuchadnezzar was content
to demand of the captive Jews, custom, toll,
and tribute, he was within his rights in the
demand, and they had no option but to pay.
But when he went beyond those recognised
limits, and demanded that they should pro-
strate themselves before his golden image,
he was trespassing within a province where

his law did not obtain, and the faithful three
were justified in saying, "Be it known unto
thee, O king, that we will not serve thy gods,
nor worship the golden image which thou
hast set up." Similarly Daniel was perfectly
justified in refusing to be bound by the king's
restriction as to prayer. "When Daniel
knew that the decree was signed, he went into
his house, and prayed and gave thanks unto
his God, as he did aforetime." If Paul had
allowed that a man must become a Jew before
he became a Christian, according to the ruling
of the Pharisees, the offence of the Cross
would have ceased, and he would not have been
subjected, first, to weary years of imprisonment, and ultimately to martyrdom. If the
early Christians had admitted that the Em-
peror was divine, and had obeyed the law to
give him divine honour, though the admission
was given in the slightest manner possible,
by scattering a few grains of incense on the

altar-fires, they would have escaped the ten
awful persecutions that swept the Empire
like prairie-fires. But they resolved that
they must, in these respects, obey God rather
than men. So is it still, there may be times
in human history when a sole ruler, or the
majority, may determine on a policy which
Conscience resents, because it conflicts with
its solemn witness to the Truth; and under
such circumstances, as Luther said, "A man
can do no other than refuse to submit, for
it is not right for a man to sin against his
conscience."

Of course, it is legitimate to leave the
country which has resolved on such demands.
The Pilgrim Fathers acted on this principle
when they crossed the ocean to found a New
England beyond the seas. On the other
hand, it may be better to stay in the country,
as the Puritans did, and suffer privations and
persecutions, until they have led it to a better

mind. But however the matter may be de-
cided, Conscience must determine our course.

It is very desirable that, where possible,
we should give time and thought to help the
State. The decisions to which the nation
comes, may be largely influenced by Christian
thought and speech. The public conscience
will recognise the voice of Truth and Righteousness, when sanely voiced by Christian
advocates. We should endeavour to transfer
as much as possible of our Lord's teaching to
the Statute-Book of the Nation to which we
belong. We should be prepared, if called upon
and moved from love of truth—but never
from motives of ambition or self-aggrandise-
ment—to give personal service to the enacting
and administering of Law. This is one of
the ways in which we can answer that great
petition : " Thy Kingdom come ! "

XVII.

THE UNIVERSAL SOLVENT.

"Love is the fulfilling of the Law."—Rom. xiii. 10.

THE Apostle has been laying down many rules and regulations for the application of Christianity to life. As we have seen, he has covered the ground pretty thoroughly, and has shown the appropriate line of conduct for each encounter; but at the close of the long enumeration he seems to say, "After all, if only you are filled with the perfect love of God, you will know exactly how to act; you will do more, you will know how to fill the measure of your opportunity to the full." The word *fulfil* means more than *fill*. It is the intensive form of *fill*.

It suggests good measure, heaped up, and
running over.

An obvious illustration of the way in which
love fulfils, is the contrast between the young
servant-girl and the wife, mother and house-
keeper. When the girl enters a household,
she has to act by rule. With some care she
is informed how to meet the various demands
of the house and home. When to rise, how
to prepare the food, the handling of the babe,
the care of the children, the management of
the kitchen, nursery, or bedroom. But if
she is married in a perfect love, she will
almost instinctively do all that she would
have previously done by obedience to rule.
She will indeed do a great deal more. Wives
and mothers will perform services for those
they love, which no money would ever pro-
cure. Night after night they will nurse the
sick child, with no thought of taking rest ;
and almost miraculously will compensate for

lack of money, food, and every appliance, on
which the mere hireling would positively
insist. In such cases Love is the fulfilling
of the Law. Not only is the soul that loves,
kept from infringing the " Thou shalt Nots "
of the Decalogue, but it fulfils the positive
commandments of the Sermon on the Mount.
Not one jot or tittle passes away from the
Law. All is fulfilled. Thus our Lord was
amply justified when He said, " I am not
come to destroy, but to fulfil."

The Apostle says Love is the debt or due
that we can never adequately discharge.
We can pay every other debt, so as to look
the whole world in the face, because we owe
nothing to any man ; but we can never look
into the face of man, woman, and child, and
feel that we have loved them enough, or done
all that love might, and ought to have done.
When we have done our utmost and best for
another, it is only an instalment, and the

great debt is hardly reduced. Moreover,
Love grows by giving. She is never satisfied.
As she gives she wants to give more. When
once she has tasted the sweetness of doing
and giving, she is always craving for larger
draughts of the intoxicating beverage of
selflessness.

The great matter with us all is to obtain
that Love.   It is the child not of the Intellect,
but of the Heart. We cannot produce it
directly by the effort of the will; but by
God's help we can put ourselves into that
position, in which the direct beam of His
nature, which is Love, may be received by
us, absorbed into us, and emitted from us.
And this is the only way to love with God's
love. When the Apostle cried, " The Love
of Christ constraineth us," he did not mean
primarily his love to Christ or Christ's love
to him, but the very Love which is the very
Heart of Christ.   There are diamonds which

have the peculiar property of absorbing the
sun's rays, so that they continue to emit
them, when carried into a dark room. So
Moses' face shone, and so Paul, after living
in the sunlight of Christ's Face, felt that his
Master's Nature had been communicated to
himself. He loved because he had been
loved, and with the love with which he had
been loved.

This is the essence of the new birth. When
we are born again, it is not that something
is born into us, but we are born into a new
world. In natural birth the child is born
into the physical round of Nature, and
begins to function among the things to which
it is introduced by its senses; and, in the
second birth, we are born into the spiritual
world, and begin to function among the
things of the Spirit. "That which is born of
the flesh is flesh, and that which is born of the
Spirit is spirit." Among the most precious

results of the natural birth is the gift of the
intellect, by which we accumulate and store
knowledge; but among the results of our
second birth into the realm of the Spirit, is
the creation within us of the clean heart and
the right spirit. "Create in me a clean
heart, O God," said David, "and renew a
right spirit within me." This is the direct
result of Regeneration. "The eyes of our
heart are opened." We no longer see men as
trees walking, but we see everything plainly.
"Therefore if any man is in Christ, he is a
new creature; old things are passed away,
behold all things are become new."

But all these things are of God. It is He
who sends forth His Spirit, and they are
created; and He renews the face of the earth.
It may be that you have been born again,
but you have not begun to use the spiritual
faculties with which you are endowed. You
are like a child, who has all the organs of

sense and the limbs of motion, but they are atrophied from disuse. Little by little they have to be brought into use, but not without effort and perhaps some twinges of pain.

Now, the one matter which demands your immediate attention is to begin to do the things which lie within the range of the spirit-life ; and the first of these is to love. You must begin to love. You say that there are people in your life that you cannot possibly *like*. But that is no answer. *Love* is not dependent on *liking*. We have to love people whom we do not like ; and the remarkable point is, that when we love in the power of our spirit-life, we end by liking the person for whom we had originally a strong antipathy.

It is well to begin with one individual within the range of our life ; because the same solution that dissolves one difficulty will settle all. (1) Begin by opening your heart to the Love of God. Be willing that the Love of God, which is certainly in His Fatherly heart towards the person in question, may have the right of way through you. *You* cannot, but *He* can. Be willing that through your lips, or hands, or mind, He should express His love to that soul. (2) Begin to pray in the spirit for it. Wait before God, till the yearning pity which dwells in Him may rise in you also, and you become aware that the living waters are issuing forth over the threshold of the inner shrine. (3) Look out for whatever is lovely in that other. Refuse to consider the wrong. If you only see wrong, it is because you are wrong; but as you persist in dwelling on the good rather than the bad, your behaviour and your feelings will undergo a complete change. It shall be as when the clear shining of a candle sheds light everywhere through the inner chamber. (4) Finally, take any opportunity of doing a service for the one from whom you have

been alienated.　You may not love from your
heart, but you can love with your strength,
and you will come to love with your mind,
your soul, and your strength.　Then you
will no longer need to be held in by the bit
and bridle of the Law, but will run in the
way of His commandments.

XVIII.

ARM, ARM, YE BRAVE.

" Put on the Armour of Light."—Rom. xiii. 11–14.

THE scene of this paragraph is gathered
from Paul's long association with
Roman soldiers. A Roman army has been
all day on the march. The sultry heat has
almost overpowered the rank and file, and the
dust raised by many feet has penetrated
through the interstices of their armour, to the
irritation of the skin. Every soldier is thankful to mark the declining sun and the lengthen-
ing shadows, which indicate the conclusion of
the day's toils, and the near approach of
welcome rest. Presently the brown tents of
the camp appear on the hillside, prepared

against their coming ; and they file in, weary
and dusty, to cast off their heavy armour, at
the word of command, and to abandon themselves to the enjoyment of well-earned rations
and repose.   Outside the tents, the men pile
their arms.   Soon the food is served and the
drink goes round ; and, perhaps, as darkness
gathers, the tents may become scenes of riot.
Under the cover of darkness, deeds are perpetrated that dare not meet the eye of day.

In the meanwhile, the sentries are at their
posts ; and when, finally, the last revellers
are silenced in slumber, and the stars look
down on the sleeping camp, no sound is heard
but their measured tread, and their challenges,
and the change of guard.   On an upper spur
of rock stands the special sentry, who eagerly
scans the Eastern sky for the first symptom
of the returning day.   Often he supposes that
the first glimmer of dawn is issuing from the
opening doors of the day, but further waiting

and watching convince him of his mistake. But at last, there is no kind of doubt. The night is far spent and the day is at hand. Lifting up his voice he cries, so that the whole sleeping camp can hear, " Comrades, it is high time to awake out of sleep, the night is departing, the day is advancing ; put off the works of darkness, and put on the armour of light."

When these words were penned, the Apostle probably was thinking of the near Advent of the Lord.   He counted time from the moment when these Roman converts had believed, and said that their full salvation, when they should greet the Christ, and be changed into His image, was coming nearer on the wings of every minute.   He urged them, therefore, to lay aside their lethargy, and awake out of the sleep that had stolen over some of them, so as to **prepare** to meet the perfect day, the excelling glory of the Master's presence.

With us the argument and appeal are somewhat different. The change has taken place within us, and is taking place more and more completely. We were darkness, but now we are light in the Lord. The god of this world had blinded the sight of our spirit, lest the light of God should shine in on us. But Christ has given us light. The darkness, which was our portion when we employed only the light of intellect, is passing, and now that we live and walk in the Spirit, we discern the things of the Spirit. We have been brought out of darkness into God's marvellous light. We are children of the light and of the day. The true Light now shineth. The glory of the Lord has arisen on us. Darkness may cover the earth, and gross darkness the peoples, but the Lord has arisen upon us, and His glory is being seen upon us. " All the children of Israel have light in their dwellings." It is hardly necessary to add, that we must put off the works of darkness, as the soldiers put off the garments and deeds, which are tolerated in their tents, but are unbecoming for the dawn.

It is most important that we should distinguish, not only between white and black, but between the different shades of grey. We must put away, not only what is clearly objectionable and evil, but whatever is doubtful. The Apostle advises us to put away, for instance, not only filthiness, but foolish talking and jesting, which are not becoming. (I do not think that this includes humour, which is one of God's great gifts, just as laughter is.) We are also bidden to lay aside every weight, as well as the sin that does so easily beset us, because there are things in our lives which are weights, if not sins. We must also desist from looking on what is a deformity in other people's characters and compel ourselves to look only on what is pleasant and beautiful—this is the divine

way of redeeming men. Bring everything to
the radiance of the inner light, which is Christ.
All things, which are reproved by that light,
must be abandoned. To him that thinketh a
thing to be unclean, to him it is unclean. The
fact that others permit it, is no reason why he
should do so. To his own Master he stands
or falls. Who art thou that judgest another
man's conscience ! The Apostle enumerates
six things of which we must specially divest
ourselves : " Let us walk honestly as in the
day ; not in revelling and drunkenness, not
in chambering and wantonness, not in strife
and jealousy."

But this is not enough to satisfy the clarion-
call of the dawn. It is not enough to doff the
works of darkness, we must don the fragrance
and beauty of the day. " Let us, since we are
of the day, be sober, putting on the breastplate of faith and love, and for a helmet,
the hope of salvation." " Let us put on the

armour of light," as when the Roman soldier placed on his person helmet, breastplate, greaves, and army-shoes, and took in hand his shield and spear—all of them carefully burnished and shining like silver, under the kiss of the morning-light.

But the more comprehensive statement of the case is in the words : " Put ye on the Lord Jesus Christ, and make no provision for the flesh, to fulfil the lusts thereof." As to the latter clause, it is sufficient to say, that all sin begins in lust, in the passionate desire of the mind, and that the main thing is simply to ignore the wrongly-directed or excessive cravings of our nature. Ignore them, refuse to listen to them, ridicule their importunity. They will not hurt you, if you are stedfastly set on that which is good, and pure, and lovely. If you cannot keep the door shut, one look of faith will bring Jesus to keep it with all the might of pure love.

But as to putting on the Lord Jesus! These words should be compared with Eph. iv. 24, which might be rendered:—Put on the new man, that new and better self, which hath been created by Christ Jesus to resemble God in the righteousness and holiness, which come from the truth. He created this better self by His life in a human body, now raised to the right hand of the Throne, and glorified with the glory He had with the Father, before the worlds were made. The phrase should also be compared with Col. iii. 10: "Put on the new man, which is being renewed unto knowledge, after the image of Him that created him." It is clear that our Saviour, by His life, death, and resurrection, has created an absolutely new type of man which each of us is called to put on, and wear as the habit and usage of daily life. In every word and act, we are to put off what savours of the old, and put on the livery of our Lord. We